ADVANCE PRAISE

This easy-reading book takes the reader through a potted history of commercial jet flight, interspersed with the personal and touching story of the author's involvement. There is a short and interesting insight into his apprenticeship in The Air Corps. The book focuses on the famous De Havilland Comet jet—what it did to transform air travel for millions, and the technical challenges that its designers had to overcome in the process of capturing the prize of "first in class."

The experiences of the author as a flight engineer throw a wonderful light on the immediate post-Second World War world, and life in the many exotic destinations that he and the Comet fleet serviced. On one of his visits to Karachi the aircraft nearly ran out of fuel attempting to land in fog, and there was a subsequent hairy diversion to a—fortunately—nearby military base.

An enjoyable read which I am pleased to recommend. The view back in time to the authors awakening to things aviation is so typical of the ways that young men and women become "hooked" on aviation. Anybody interested in the way of the world in those years would do well to read and note the many social observations and cultural nuances, some of which have followed through the decades and escalated into formidable forces of international reach and import. It's an enjoyable and insightful read and carries much within its pages by way of social history and comment.

PAUL FRY

Brigadier General OC Air Corps (Retired)

I really enjoyed your book and your recollections of your days in the early aviation business-- and especially the early life of jet-age commercial air transport. Your experiences in getting qualified on the Comet were very interesting and provided a glimpse of what life was when we were first exploring really long-distance jet transportation. I also really loved the story of how you met and courted your wife!

JOHN HEARING

Systems Engineering Manager

Boeing Co.

With the perspective of one born before Lindberg's *Spirit of Saint Louis* touched down in Paris, I still find soaring into the sky in a huge metal machine to be something of a miracle. In flight, I often have an intense curiosity about the mysterious activities in the cockpit. *Venture into the Stratosphere* took me into the cockpit to observe the crew carrying out their duties. I learned how they interact in times of boredom and in times of sheer terror. I learned what they want to inform me about, and what they want to conceal from me. I found out how their passionate dedication to advanced technologies and constant travel affect their private lives.

It is a "must" read for those who find the airplane to be a magic carpet for exploring the earth and who love flying as I do.

ANTONINUS WALL

President (Emeritus), Dominican School for Philosophy and Theology,

Graduate Theological Union. Berkeley.

I was honored to be selected to be one of the first to read and review Dominic Colvert's book *Venture into the Stratosphere: Flying the First Jet Liners.*

Living in Miami Springs all of my young life, I was exposed to every one of the earlier Airlines—Eastern, Pam American, National etc. *Venture into the Stratosphere* touches on the personal experience and hands-on venture of Dominic's aviation career—his personal eye-opening trials and experiences, and his climb through the ranks from the aviation units into the engineering field; then finally into the cockpit.

As an aviator of fifty years, an Expert Witness Consultant, a Designated Pilot Examiner (DPE) of the Federal Aviation Administration (FAA), and Flight Instructor Glider and Aerobatic Glider, I recommend this readable book. It gives good insight into the early airliners in the United Kingdom, the thrills and difficulty in advancement of British Overseas Airway Corporation (BOAC), and early United Kingdom aviation through Dominic's eyes.

SHAWN KNICKERBOCKER

FAA ATP ASEL, ASES, AMEL, AMES, Rotorcraft-Helicopter

Flight Instructor, ASE, AME, CFII Airplane, Rotorcraft-Helicopter,

CFII Helicopter and Glider

FAA NVG Certified CFI

Transport Canada Aviation Authority (TCAA) ATP ASEL, ASES, AMEL, AMES

Venture Into The Stratosphere

VENTURE
INTO THE
STRATOSPHERE

FLYING THE FIRST JETLINERS

DOMINIC COLVERT

NEW YORK

LONDON • NASHVILLE • MELBOURNE • VANCOUVER

Venture Into The Stratosphere

Flying the First Jetliners

Published in New York, New York, by Morgan James Publishing. Morgan James is a trademark of Morgan James, LLC. www.MorganJamesPublishing.com

The Morgan James Speakers Group can bring authors to your live event. For more information or to book an event visit The Morgan James Speakers Group at www.TheMorganJamesSpeakersGroup.com.

ISBN 9781683507932 paperback
ISBN 9781683507949 eBook
Library of Congress Control Number: 2017915676

Design by:
Celac Colvert

In an effort to support local communities, raise awareness and funds, Morgan James Publishing donates a percentage of all book sales for the life of each book to Habitat for Humanity Peninsula and Greater Williamsburg.

Get involved today! Visit
www.MorganJamesBuilds.com

DEDICATION

To
CATHERINE ANN

ACKNOWLEDGEMENTS

Writing memoirs quickly brings one face-to-face with the poet's (John Donne) sentiment, "no man is an island." I could see that the love and sacrifice of family, and that later the generosity of friends, too numerous to mention, in The Air Corps and BOAC were essential to any successes I had. But in bringing the present work to fruition I should first thank my sons, Celac and Gavin, not just for support, but for the inspiration they provided. I also owe a special thanks to Dr. Jennifer at FirstEditing.com for her attention to detail and for valuable suggestions in consonance with the style and tone of the work. Finally I want to thank the Morgan James Publishing team; David Hancock, CEO and Founder, has created a uniquely helpful system that treats authors as valuable partners. Terry Whalen believed in my project and greatly encouraged me to finish the manuscript and develop a proposal, while Aubrey Kosa, Gayle West, and Bethany Marshall were guides to making the difficult production and marketing process as seamless as possible.

CONTENTS

PREFACE

I had occasion recently to forage through some old records from my past. There among them lay my flight log book. I was pleased and amazed by my son Celac's reaction to it—he saw it as a virtual treasure. And as we thumbed through it, he was eager to see the entry for a remarkable flight that I had recounted to him when he was a young boy. The stark, cryptic entries in the book were a key to times and places no longer in commonplace experience!

The aviation technology of 1958 was an outgrowth of World War Two, and it bears clear kinship with today's more advanced airplanes. It was also the beginning of the jet age for passengers. These jetliners, in effect, shrank the world and produced social changes that, up to now, have not been well studied.

Also, we ascribe something magical to beginnings, so I happily promised to recapture, for my grandchildren and others, my challenges and excitement of that era. But there is a broader consideration: something akin to a duty, to record the history of a period that was the root of significant worldwide change.

History is charged with telling us who we are, and what actually happened. The case has been made in the recent past that there is a dichotomy between these two things; between the myth, that is, the symbols and source of our world view, and the Historical Critical Method (HCM). However, a good story serves both giving facts in relevant context. With emphasis on the *good* story it is important that the context illuminates the facts and not be selected for ideological purposes. The good story also leads to trans-historical meaning. It speaks to the big questions, such as the purposes of our present lives.

Venture into the Stratosphere is a history of the excitement and challenges in flying the first jetliners. The explanation of these events is, not a recounting of raw facts, but a voyage in a hugely diverse world. The illumination of that world touches upon, say, gyroscopic instruments, a love story, social interactions, engineering philosophy, war-time conditions, and on and on.

The trans-historical meaning in the story has to be a function of what an individual reader brings to its appraisal. However, the striving, innovation, and, what I call, the sacrificial daring of early aviators, will be very inspirational.

CHAPTER ONE

THE ELIXIR OF FREEDOM

My earliest interest in flying machines was in 1939. I never saw those behemoths—the airships—that preceded the flying boats in ferrying passengers across the Atlantic. But in 1939, when silver machines were spotted in the sky in our airspace in County Tipperary, everyone was excited and stopped to gaze heavenward. The adults' excitement was contagious; and we, little kids, ran around with our arms extended, yelling "Yankee Clipper! Yankee Clipper!" For that was what our mentors had identified the object in the sky to be. You might think "cute, but not a powerful story." However, remember that scarcely a generation earlier, the idea of a silver machine flying through the air could only have occurred in Greek mythology.

In a short time, make-believe Yankee Clipper gave way to exploring our rural surroundings. I remember my brother Brendon organized an expedition to *An Cnoc.* This was a hill from which we were promised to see parts of *seven* counties "on a clear day." It was an all-day trek, so we started early. Armed with stout sticks and with our commander reconnoitering the route we, budding Roald Amundsens, strode through fields, walked carefully around fairy forts, hurried past paddocks that might have dangerous bulls, gave wide berth to farmers' houses with their inevitable watchdogs, and paused to pick blackberries and whorts (whortleberries) as the opportunities arose.[1] By midday, we were ascending the final steep climb to the summit. Triumphant and seated in that commanding position, we, with some misgivings, hungrily downed our lunch rations purloined from the kitchen. The misgivings arose because it had been thought in the morning that adequate rations for the trip included some of Auntie Maie's raisins. It must be remembered that this was war time and any imported goods, such as raisins, were an extreme rarity. I will never know how Auntie Maie got them, but I know she planned a scrumptious and rare cake.

At the summit, my knowledge of geography and terrestrial science did not permit me to identify for sure the *terra firma* of seven counties. Nevertheless, it was a satisfying experience. The return journey was tough and we were tired when we reached home. I expected dire consequences from Auntie Maie. She brought up the subject and Brendon shouldered full responsibility for the irreplaceable raisins. He pleaded necessity. She was a gentle lady and, to my continued amazement, she accepted my brother's plea, without admitting to his military necessity part. We were experiencing how the distaff side of the house primed boys to be men!

On the long days of summer vacation, my brother, Terry, and I worked as a team, savoring the pleasure of fishing in streams too tiny to have a name. We would bring home our catch of trout that was six inches or bigger. Our prize catch was a marvelous eighteen-inch specimen, taken from the head springs of the river closest to us. After the heads were cut off and they were gutted, Mama pan fried them. Those fish had a deliciousness never again, in my experience, to be equaled. Although we did fish with rod and line—using worms for bait, and a hook crudely fashioned from Mama's sewing supplies—it was the elemental nature of hand fishing that made it our much-loved challenge. The contemplative experience of sitting on the river bank waiting for a fish to bite faded in comparison to removing boots and socks, wading into the stream, and attempting to outwit the wily fish.

The crowning experience for "The Young Lads of the River" was the legendary trout of Kyle that got away.[2] Kyle was a place about a mile beyond the village and there, hidden in a sheltered ravine, was a small year-round unnamed river. We discovered the enormous trout that inhabited an impregnable pool in that river. We thought of him in the singular, though *he* was undoubtedly just one of many. Here was a challenge we could not refuse! On a hot day, we entered the overgrown ravine and headed upstream through the dappled sunlight. In less than a half mile we arrived at the pool; it was at the base of a waterfall. The glinting waters at the top of the falls plummeting ten or twelve feet had sculpted out a very deep pool at the base. The aerated water at the base flowed out into a progressively shallower, dark, limpid pool for about thirty or forty feet before the river returned to an ankle-depth, burbling stream among the rocks.

So we devised our plan of attack. We knew the secret of hand fishing—the hands must be placed motionless in the water until the fish approaches close enough that it cannot escape. The slightest movement alerts the fish to danger and he darts away; in this case upstream into the inaccessible deep. So, we rolled up our shorts and waded in above knee height into the shockingly cold water. The shaded pool water was close to ground temperature, definitely less than fifty degrees. Facing toward the shallows, we hold our hands steady in the water, and wait for *him* to appear. We did not last very long, and gave up as hands and legs became painfully numb, and a deep blue color from the icy cold water. However, we did not surrender easily. We returned a number of times to the contest, but the quarry always managed to elude us and flee to his mysterious sanctuary.

In competitive games, I liked handball and practiced my skills endlessly against any convenient gable wall. Running held great interest for all of us and we secretly envisioned, if it were humanly possible, our being the first to run the four-minute mile. Remember, it was to be 1954 before this worldwide interest in the sub-four-minute mile was resolved by Roger Bannister. We were also inspired by the performance of John Joe Barry (The Ballincurry Hare) of Kyle, who actually—not to our surprise—went on to hold many world- class records for running.

We committed ourselves to investigating beyond the horizon, beyond the visible more distant features of the landscape—Slievenamon and the Devils Bit. We were not going to set any limits to our horizons. *The silver machine in the sky was the sign of another even more exciting dimension of the world awaiting exploration.* We would venture into the stratosphere. Indeed our youthful spirits were fired up with the excitement, not just for geographic discovery, but also for the potential for a holistic knowledge of the cosmos.

We tasted the ultimate in freedom. Of course, if you had asked us the meaning of freedom we could not have answered. Nor did we analyze the aphorisms we imbibed from our widowed mother that emphasized that we should fearlessly seek the *objective* truth. It would require more maturity to see objectivity as the elixir of freedom. Referring to the Jeffersonian compendium of the good life, it could be said that we were grateful for the gift of life and freedom that produced happiness. But this exercise of freedom was not in any passing pleasure; for Mama's rules were strict, and we could see, for example, that those "given to drink" were enslaved. Instead, we thought to pursue the good as a kind of inchoate natural law. For me, the sense of freedom and wellbeing was often acute at the end of a busy day when the shades of sleep would envelop my tired body. As the demands of the external world faded, without conceptualization, the pure experience of *Being* produced a euphoria before sleep enveloped the mind.

I was, however, a veteran of the jet age before I had an opportunity to explore the aircraft that was the summit of flying boat technology— the Yankee Clipper, or more exactly, the Boeing B-314. Construction of an airport for seaplanes at Foynes on the Shannon River began in 1935. The airport, being on neutral territory in World War Two, became one of the world's largest civilian airports in the 1940s. It served worldwide destinations and the huge flying boats took off from there on the initial trans-Atlantic routes. After the flying boat era came to an end and the land-based planes moved to Rineanna (now Shannon) airport, a marvelous exhibit was built at the Foynes museum: floating in its own lagoon, is a B-314 built from Boeing's original blue prints.

Exploring the interior of this "Yankee Clipper," was indeed a wondrous venture. You can wander about the Boeing's B-314's spacious cabin interior; you can envisage poring over the maps in mid-Atlantic at the navigator station, or hauling back on the control column to nudge the boat from the Shannon River into the air.

For me, the childhood thrill of aviation never really wore off. In our school library, I delighted in books on adventure and travel to mysterious places. I read about and identified with heroes like Charles Lindbergh and Amelia Earhart. I harbored dreams of travel to far-off mysterious places and to see and understand the whole breadth of human existence.

By the time I reached manhood, coming from a strong family, I had a positive self image. So, the Western ideas in my upbringing would be the position from which I would examine the civics and cultures of those mysterious places I would visit. I would naturally scrutinize things for their conformance to the concept of freedom, which was a palpable part of our existence. This sentiment, as distinct from the practice, related immediately to the French Revolution but ultimately came through turbulent history from more ancient times.[3] As epitomized in the American Revolution, Western nations hearkened to the cry for freedom, and the eighteenth and nineteenth centuries saw the borders and civic dynamics of Europe change. England and other countries, of course, would remain colonial powers for some time, but their internal politics were democratic. Even in England, where the Head of State and the Head of State Church are *ceremonially* one and the same person, and bishops sat in the House of Lords, there was freedom of conscience.

Ireland, in the 1950's, had recently passed through a tumultuous period. Only a generation had passed since its terrifying civil war. Prior to that, in common with other European nations, the country also had a history of civil, cultural, and religious struggles that lived vividly in the people's memory. The mark of those historical exertions was to leave our minds cherishing these symbols: separation of spiritual and civic powers, democracy, and freedom. The separation of powers was essentially a part of the Irish Christian heritage that guaranteed the treasured freedom of conscience.[4]

However, by the 1950s, these higher things belonged to a vaguely held or unspoken philosophy. My concerns were naturally directed toward economic possibilities, and to choosing a successful career in line with my youthful aspirations.

CHAPTER TWO

MASTERY OF THE AIR

o understand the thrill aviation held for society in general in those early days, it is necessary to transpose oneself in spirit to that bygone era. This is no easy task, given that we now routinely fly to a destination to accomplish something *there*. Furthermore, the experience of *getting there* may be for us no more than a distraction from our computer or the entertainment system movie channel. Imagine, though, the wonderful experience when for the airplane passenger *getting there* was still a first class adventure!

From prehistory, people were mindful of heavier-than-air flight. The powerful and graceful flights of many species of birds always excited envy and dreams of human aviation: as in the Biblical expression where Isaiah says, "they will soar as with eagles' wings." The human spirit was uplifted even by a mental image of a bird's eye view that was so often captured by the creativity of an artist, and, after October 1783, by those privileged to make an ascent in a hot air balloon. For such earth-bound people, actual aviation was a savoring of the magic of bi-location.

Those ancient dreams are celebrated in the Greek myth of Icarus, who escaped Crete on wings constructed by his father with wax and feathers. Glorying in his freedom and driven by hubris, Icarus flies too high. Being too close to the sun the wax melts and he crashes and drowns in the Icarian Sea. In true mythical fashion, the story is more than mere fantasy, and these twin themes—happiness and hubris—were still marks of heavier-than-air flight in the 1930s and 1950s.

Nothing better demonstrates the widespread—may we say, universal—appreciation of the human venture into the air than the frenzied emotional adulation poured out worldwide on Charles Lindbergh's daring, but foolhardy, flight from New York to Paris in 1927. On May 21st, when he made landfall at Dingle Bay in Ireland, and while traversing southern England and Normandy, people rushed from their houses to wave to him. At Paris, he was greeted by a mob of admirers a hundred thousand strong. But these demonstrations were only a beginning; the outpouring of approval for the man and his achievement was truly international. Effusive demonstrations were made in Belgium, England, Mexico, Japan, and China.[5] While Lindbergh, the man, was later to suffer rejection, his achievement in that first New York to Paris flight never lost its appeal. It was estimated that an astonishing 25 percent of the American population turned out to greet him and laud his success.

Probably the first *routine* manned heavier-than-air flights were achieved in California by a University of Santa Clara professor, John J. Montgomery, in glider flights from 1883 to 1911. Following the earth-shattering 1906 San Francisco earthquake, Montgomery's experiments were held up. On resumption of his experiments, he was killed in

October 1911 when his glider stalled and crashed. At Kitty Hawk in December 1903, the Wright brothers achieved their renowned take-off, and first sustained manned heavier-than-air flight using an internal combustion power plant.

These wonderful achievements in the technology and art of flying unleashed, as we have noted, a natural human interest and delight in aviation. But what was to be the commercial aspects of these innovations? There was money to be made in air shows and demonstrations of death-defying feats. Charles Lindbergh recounts that on his first parachute jump he decided it would be a "double jump." When he exited the airplane his canopy blossomed, then he collapsed it. As he was falling free, the crowd gasped at witnessing a man falling to his death. Then he opened a second parachute. But such circuses were by nature not going to be truly large businesses unless they involved the general public in a useful way, and as more than just spectators.

It so happened, that nineteenth-century institution, the Post Office, was the key to commercialization. There was a market for the value received from air mail—a high-value lightweight payload. Commerce is, of course, stimulated by prompt communications. But more importantly, in human terms, as a social reality, the harshness of being separated from those we love is softened by speedy exchanges. In America, the Post Office proved to be a vital component of the westward migration. Without its delivery of letters and newspapers an American *national* politics was hardly conceivable.

The early aircraft flights in the mail business competed with horse-drawn, automotive, and steam train postal services on land, and with telegraph messaging. In this environment, the revenues from air mail were able to attract entrepreneurial capital. Mail contracts have been a vital part of aviation economics from the earliest days to the jet age.

Where it was difficult to attract brave passengers, a Post Office air mail subsidy could turn a profit.

Remarkably, the first east-bound non-stop crossing of the Atlantic in 1919 carried a mail satchel. John Alcock and Arthur Brown carried it in their modified Vickers Vimy aircraft, flying from St. John's, Newfoundland to a crash landing in Clifden, Ireland—where they mistook a soft water-logged bog for an open grassy field. They proudly delivered the satchel in London a few days later, despite the unplanned events. Alcock and Brown's speed of delivery was well beyond any possible surface competing services.

In the years 1914 to 1918, the war effort for World War One became the impetus to greatly advance the use of aircraft. Beginning with, in military terms, incredibly valuable reconnaissance flights, the ace fighter pilots became as the knights of old: legendary heroes ever ready for gladiatorial combat and a high-minded respect for their antagonists. After the war, there was wide spread admiration for the flyers and the many achievements in aviation. By the 1930s, improvements too numerous to mention made aircraft like the Yankee Clipper possible. There were advances in the theory of flight; mechanical instrumentation; radio instrumentation; more powerful types of fuel; and in stronger, more durable, lightweight construction. Of particular importance was the development of powerful aircraft radial engines and variable pitch, fully feathering propellers.

The value of engines of increased power-to-weight ratio is readily understandable, but the importance of *feathering* is not as obvious. Feathering, in aviation, as in rowing a boat, is the action of twisting the leading edge of the propeller, or oar, parallel to the slipstream, thus minimizing drag. Imagine a Boeing B-314 losing power in one of its four engines, then the remaining three engines would have to propel the aircraft and, of course, overcome the drag of the idled propeller. Fully feathering propellers were mechanical wonders, central to the safe operation of multiengine aircraft.

All the improvements contributed to the efficiency and effectiveness of the aircraft. But more important to aviation was the unquantifiable— accidents that did not happen—safety factor of flight. While it was still the era of the daredevil aviator, flying as a passenger by the 1930s was definitely adventurous, but not plain foolhardy.

It would take a whole literature to convey an appreciation of the horrors of war, or even some single aspects of war, such as the million-man casualty of World War One's Battle of the Somme, or of the horror of World War Two's firebombing of German cities. A person's private experience was, of course, limited; and my kind of experience, was undoubtedly endlessly repeated. I recall my aunts discussing their sister, Ettie's, heartbreaking experiences in 1918. Ettie lived in London with her sisters, her husband being away in the merchant marines. I can still hear her sisters, shielding their sadness and guilt, agree darkly, "I told her to wear warm clothing." The Germans were the first to bring the terror of the front line to a city population; they sent night-time Zeppelin bombing raids on London. My aunts blamed the bombing and the frenzied search for shelter in the London Underground for the pneumonia and tuberculosis that caused Ettie's early death.

Toward the end of World War One, in 1918, the world was struck with the greatest influenza pandemic ever. Some estimate that it killed up to 100,000,000 persons world wide—much greater than the war casualties. In the popular imagination, it was twinned with the fourteenth-century bubonic plague known as the Black Death, and thought to be, in some unknown fashion, directly connected to the war. Stories abounded of the startling brutality of the disease—a young healthy adult stricken in mid-stride and suffocating to death within hours, a general store with three of its five young shop assistants stricken dead.

World War Two saw a huge expansion of the importance of aviation to war efforts. The flying aces in fighter aircraft and the brave crewmen in heavy bombers revolutionized the nature of warfare. These aircraft were land based and an infrastructure had to be created for their deployment. As hostilities ended in 1945, the new infrastructure and the bomber technology were foundational to a civil transportation system. With new airfields and runways close to population centers, the era of the flying boat came to an end.

That war is considered to be the deadliest military conflict in history, with possibly 80,000,000 deaths from conflict and war-related famine and disease. Survivors, both demobilized soldiers and civilians, had their memories. In Europe the nights of the war years in the 1940s were often pierced by the mournful wailing of the air raid sirens. On jumping from bed, one was confronted by the surreal scene of the night sky stabbed by waving searchlights. Hurriedly one made a beeline for what safety was provided by a hastily built refuge. For those who survived, the routine could be repeated many times, and one's disposition and sanity suffered.

CHAPTER THREE

THE ETHOS OF POST-WAR AVIATION

With the signing of the armistice in 1945, the *general psyche*, though it averted to intense memories of two destructive wars and a cruel pandemic, was generally optimistic. This is not to deny the turmoil and conflict generated by social upheaval and new intellectual ideas. But we had escaped history. The futility and loss of life's meaning in a world at war would be no more. Peace is not just an absence of violence: it is a spirit of concord! Leavened by this moral triumph, poverty and health care were no more than problems to be solved. In addition, there was a positive relief that there was not a repeat of the 1918 influenza pandemic. The combination of relief and hope created a sense of, if not a utopia, a new age dawning.

Scientism was a strong force in the popular imagination, but the pessimistic theories of Malthus and other "dismal" scientists of the nineteenth century were by that time no more than academic meanderings—the depressing mathematical calculation that the dynamics of human reproduction and food production made inevitable either catastrophic war, uncontrollable disease, or widespread famine, was no longer influential. Nor was the overall consciousness yet infected by the twentieth-century pseudo-scientific Gnostic prophets of doom; "nuclear winter" of the 1950s, "silent spring" of the 1960s, and the "population bomb" of the 1970s were in the future. It seems the utopian politics of the day had not yet generated the levels of resentment, victimhood, and activism that were evident in later generations. There was in fact, a certain exuberance in the air, and people were enthusiastic about the good that aviation could accomplish. There was a continuance of the pre-war "romance of flight."

It seems with the end of hostilities, the national pride of all countries was awakened, as they scrambled to be part of the growing aviation industry. Large amounts of capital were spent from national treasuries to fund infrastructure, airlines, and passenger routes worldwide. And competition to have the most beautiful, glamorous stewardesses, the most renowned equipment, the finest meals, and the most convenient schedules was the order of the day. A cloak of heroism clung to the aircrews flying the iconic aircraft, such as: the Lockheed Constellations and Boeing Stratocruisers. Neglecting the evidence that, in general, enchantment is associated with flying, it can be said, in this case, that a widespread spirit of adventure and delight in the new possibilities for human aviation gripped a people who had suffered the ravages of two wars.

My experience could illustrate the spirit of the times. Cousin Maureen married a soldier during World War Two. They lived together for *three weeks*, and then her lover, Lance Corporal Anthony Hennessey, had to depart for frontline service. He was dead within days of arriving at the beachhead in Anzio in Italy, and was buried there with 1,055 of his comrades. After the war, she accepted the unkindness of fate and devotedly raised *their* daughter in a close and happy family. She only considered marriage again many, many years later.

Auntie Florence was the inveterate traveler of our family. Her postcards from the European tourist spots between the world wars were, for us children, windows on the great wide world. When she was home for the holidays at Christmas, Easter, and the August bank holiday, we listened with big ears, but not fully comprehending, the adults as they discussed the scenes and journeys by boats and trains and buses. During World War Two, she made the London-to- Tipperary journey for thrice-yearly visits home. Listening to her talk of rushing, queuing, waiting, standing, hauling luggage, being crowded, hungry, subject to motion sickness, and other exigencies of such travel, we thought it exotic and exciting. I think she felt a sense of accomplishment.

As air travel became more commonplace, she rejected it entirely. She certainly did not suffer from a malady such as acrophobia, vertigo, or fear of falling; but she was absolutely clear about the unsuitability of air travel. She was of a feminine character well known to Irish men—as we would say "strong minded." However, she also suffered some age-related physical maladies. Arthritis, undoubtedly exacerbated by the wartime midnight trips to damp air raid shelters, now made the odyssey to Tipperary by London underground, train, boat, shanks mares, and taxi impractical. She agreed to an airline trip, if I accompanied her.

I got her a reservation for a window seat on an Aer Lingus flight from London to Dublin. The aircraft was a Vickers Viscount, the first turboprop to enter passenger service. A window seat had her sitting next to an amazingly huge 26-inch by 19-inch window. Her first flying experience was to be on a new generation of flying machines. Aircraft with piston engines normally positioned themselves at the end of the runway and ran the engines at full takeoff power. While the aircraft vibrated madly and shuddered against the brakes, many new or hesitant passengers were thus imbued with a lack of confidence. With the Viscount's powerful Rolls Royce Dart engines, there was a seamless surge forward for takeoff. In flight, Dart engines substituted smooth operation and whining noise for the high noise levels and vibration that piston engines would have caused.

As we settled into our seats, the usually voluble lady had nothing to say. After top-of-climb we were served our food trays. On the wooden trays, overlaid with a delicate paper doily, was a light repast on china plates. In accord with the spirit of the day and the wide acceptance of smoking, each tray had a specialist airline gift pack of four cigarettes. The trays were followed by the legendary flight attendant inquiry, "Coffee, tea, or milk?" Over the food we managed some small talk, but her acceptance of the experience hung in the balance. As the charming stewardesses collected our trays and announced, "extinguish your cigarettes," the Irish coast, Dublin Bay and Howth Head, were spectacularly in view from about twenty-thousand feet through the enormous windows. "Are we really moving," she asked happily as we imperceptibly edged over the coast line for our approach to Collinstown (later Dublin) airport—then I could tell the magic of aviation had won, even with an older generation "settled in their ways."

CHAPTER FOUR

A MILITARY CAREER

I n the 1950s aviation was, as we have described, at the frontier of human experiences. However, aviation was then also at the frontier of technology. In general, while young women were drawn to understanding how the world worked in a social sense, young men were entranced by how the world worked in the physical sense. The young male mind was excited to know arcane things such as, that the left-foot pedal on a bicycle has a left-hand thread to keep it from unwinding during normal operation. What young man of those days did not dream of owning an old jalopy for the purpose of repairing it? I was also challenged by theoretical questions such as, how force at a distance was possible or the nature of radio waves. In practical things, I got my hands on radios and electrical equipment, and I read—avidly—repair manuals for automobiles I would never even see.

But I had another driving influence: my grandfather, Thomas Wall, a village schoolmaster. He died eight years before I was born, so I knew him only by reputation, but we can turn to Oliver Goldsmith's *Village Schoolmaster* for a description that rings true:

> *...The love he bore to learning was in fault,*
> *The village all declar'd how much he knew*
> *'Twas certain he could write, and cipher too:*
> *Lands he could measure, terms and tides presage....*
>
> *...And still they gaz'd and still the wonder grew,*
> *That one small head could carry all he knew....*

My schoolmaster grandfather was of a remarkably similar strength of mind. His wholehearted commitment to learning was fostered under the severe tutelage of a former hedge schoolmaster to whom, on the completion of primary school, he was apprenticed at age 14—that is, he had the job called *monitor* in a multi-class school room. A hedge school was an open-air clandestine school in Ireland when education was forbidden under the Penal laws, particularly in the seventeenth and eighteenth centuries. They retained the name, "hedge school," even as many of them were later housed in churches.

Thomas' influence on pupils was such, that sixty years after his authority had vanished they continued to write the copperplate script he would approve of. Beside his primary-school activities, he had his surveyor chains and his etching equipment for other work in his spare time. He was, of course, an autodidact, kept a journal, wrote speeches, and conversed with the learned. He found time to tutor seminary students in Latin and Greek.

However, he should not be thought of as a unique instance of a devotee of learning, but, rather, an exemplar of a tradition in the Celtic culture. Latin and Greek were taught in hedge schools, and we should note that Goldsmith's model for the poem was in all likelihood Thomas *Paddy* Byrne. Grandfather's reputation alone ensured that all his grandchildren had an impetus to education. So, I not being located near a high school, studied by correspondence courses.

The confluence of these things was that, when the Irish Army Air Corps advertized for men to train as aircraft technicians it looked like an opportunity. Here would be the romance of aviation, the attraction of technology, and the opportunity for continued education. Since positions were limited, the recruiting process required an interview, and a wait to be called, if one was successful. At my interview in Dublin, Captain Carroll asked what I did. I explained that I was an apprentice electrician installing wiring in old houses. Then he probed to see if I was curious enough to have acquired a broader knowledge. He was satisfied with my entrepreneurial spirit, as I eagerly described the Irish national electrical distribution system: generating sources and voltages at each level of distribution. I could have given more details—described the star-delta circuits, lengths of the insulators, the types of pylons, and more. But I had said enough; I instinctively knew his decision was favorable.

In military terms, history is the keeper of esprit de corps, but recent Irish politics had made history in the 1950s a contentious subject, and best left unexplored. Nationalist sentiment was heroically expressed by earlier generations in *God Save Ireland,* a song that was the *de facto* national anthem at the turn of the century.

> *God save Ireland cries the hero*
> *God save Ireland cry we all*

Whether on scaffold high or on battlefield we die
Oh what matters when for Ireland dear we fall.

The sentiment worked well in the fight for freedom, but was out of place for the civil war that followed. The generation preceding our recruits experienced deadly internecine violence, where the noble sentiment of sacrificing one's life for the common good had to be subsumed into a war of brother against brother.

The living memories of the civil war made it impossible for the Army Air Corps to use history for morale building. It was some time before I learned such things as the Air Corps was born in 1922 to provide a stealth operation that would rescue, if necessary, the Sinn Féin plenipotentiaries to the freedom talks with the British Government; that the nascent organization suffered a mutiny in 1924; and that the Army Air Corps pilot, James Fitzmaurice, was awarded the DFC (Distinguished Flying Cross) for the iconic first west-bound heavier-than-air flight crossing of the North Atlantic in 1928.

However, the Corps managed to instill a fine spirit that pushed us beyond routine—in demeanor, "look your own height;" in responsibility, "do not be satisfied with the routine, but strive for the best possible outcome." We were given instruction in many aspects of aircraft maintenance: power plant, airframes, electrical equipment, and instrumentation. Radio systems were then outside the scope of the initial training.

Not alone did most of the airmen (technicians) make every effort for a superior outcome, but, of course, the command structure supported it. Some escapades of Frank Desmond and myself give an illustration of that fine spirit. I recounted these in an article I wrote for the Army magazine:[6]

Frank and I met for the first time while attending the NCO training programme. We were both electricians and that was enough of a common interest to throw us together. Frank had an enormous zest for life and the escapades we got into quickly increased our friendship. Toward the end of the training, we were brought on maneuvers to [the] Wicklow [mountains]....

The more artistic of our group in the camp put together a show to be presented on a Sunday night. Practicing their leadership skills they divided the labour and put their limited time into creating a masterpiece production....

Frank and I had not been directly involved in the stage production. We had occupied our little spare time with trekking in the ruggedly beautiful mountains. Still, Frank, true to form, had kept an eye on what was going on in the world of theatre, while I concentrated on mountaineering. Anyway, the director discovered a major problem when the footlights in the theatre would not work. Of course, neither the actors or production crew were worried, they were confident Frank and I could resolve the complexities of the electrical system. On investigation we found, to our chagrin, that it was not an electrical problem—*there was no wiring.*

After a search we found, strung between two buildings, the one set of service wires which were not connected to a load. There, serving no purpose, was more than a hundred feet of cable, swaying in the breeze. Without a doubt it was a needless waste of good conductors as far as the camp electrical system was concerned. We speculated that this was a forgotten circuit among miles of army aerial wires....

After evening meal, with darkness approaching, we reconnoitered the scene of operations. The cables were connected at the supply side and were "hot." However, with Frank's emotional and physical support I scaled the heights and cut the cables free with an insulated pliers. We rolled the cables up and scurried to the theatre with our booty. With our new supplies in hand we had the footlights wired and operating for the evening's rehearsals....

Monday morning was spent preparing a hillside defense.... We unwillingly expended large amounts of energy on the hard stony ground, to fashion what our sergeant would agree was a military trench. My fatigue at lunch time was compounded by a sinking feeling when Frank told me the camp's Board of Works superintendent had spotted the missing cables. He also knew the two guys with whom he wished to discuss the problem. To say he spotted the missing cables is not entirely accurate—*how could he not miss the cables that ran to his office?* He had hoped to complete the hook-up when the services of an electrician became available. The completed wiring would give light and heat to the office on those cold winter evenings.

A few discreet inquiries on the superintendent's part had named the culprits of the "missing service cables" crime. Although Board of Works staff are civilians, the superintendent showed a clear understanding of the unwritten army law concerning equipment. He declared, "If the cables are relocated to their original place nothing further will be said."

Unfortunately, the average distance between stage footlights is around 12 to 18 inches and that was the average length of the pieces of cable after Frank and I had concluded our work on the stage. Nothing short of Divine Intervention could meet the superintendent's dictum....

That afternoon we hunkered down in our rather shallow trenches.... In the midst of the bedlam Frank slithered into my trench. To this day I cannot imagine how he did it! He had described our predicament to an Ordinance NCO and convinced him that a further relocation of army property was in order. The deal was this: the Ordinance guys would be slow in removing a certain portion of the detonation cables used for the plastic charges. Frank and I could "acquire" what we needed—no questions asked....

Installing the new cables was a more difficult and dangerous job than removing the old ones. Stringing the cables was easy for me but making the live connections while clinging perilously with one hand and carefully twisting the wires together was another matter. We lacked any form of mechanical connector to make the connections, and had to be satisfied with the twisted joints....

Of course, mature reflection tells me that I was mistaken in thinking that the whole incident was hidden from the command structure. Undoubtedly, whatever action they saw as "contrary to good order and military discipline" they balanced in their military scales with "initiative...."

CHAPTER FIVE

IRISH ARMY AIR CORPS

I n the almost six years I spent in military service, there were, of course, military duties such as parades, guard duty, fire arms training, and so on. But the primary experience was an exposure to aviation from the trivial to the exotic. Our identity and self-worth were enmeshed in achieving military and civilian certifications as aircraft technicians.

My introduction to engine technology in 1952 consisted of being given a defunct engine and access to discarded parts to assemble a complete power plant. Our little team of four budding aircraft mechanics, approached this challenge with much seriousness and attention to detail. Such keen dedication was rewarded with the opportunity to fit our reconstructed engine with a propeller, and run it up to power in a test bed. We were prouder than peacocks!

Airframe technology had seen great advances. The Wright brothers had flown what was, in essence, a kite. Subsequent successful designs used the same construction techniques. Rods and bracing wires made the shape and strength of aerofoil and fuselage components, the surfaces of which were covered with canvas stiffened with dope. Since the early airframe maintenance consisted largely of adjusting the bracing wires, the mechanics who did that were known as riggers. In our rigger course work, we had to produce a number of proper cable splices. Airframes, by that time, were designed like a chicken egg, where the strength of the structure is in the stressed skin. In these modern structures, called monocoque or semi-monocoque, only the aircraft control cables still required rigging.

The Army Air Corps had *ab initio* trainers, aircraft for coastal patrol, twin-engine multipurpose passenger aircraft, and helicopters for search and rescue. During my time there, I worked on the following aircraft: Miles Magister, de Havilland Chipmunk, Hawker Hurricane, Supermarine Spitfire, Percival Provost, de Havilland Vampire, Avro Anson, and de Havilland Dove. Apart from the work with aircraft, I also gained priceless experience in refurbishing, from the ground up, my old jalopy.

I was stationed at Gormanstown Camp for a period, where the Air Corps did their initial pilot training. There I had charge of the Electrical Shop, and was a part-time ground instructor to the cadet pilots. The sergeant I replaced there, had left his old vehicle behind when discharged from the service. It sat on a little hillock, grass and weeds spurting from under its flat tires and poking through the engine compartment. Its license plates, IM2617, were still readable, but its green paint work had turned to brown rust around the bottom. The ex-sergeant and I struck a bargain: I became the insecure owner of an immobile car, and he agreed to receive £30 in installments.

There is an often-quoted *metaphysical law of travel*: "the more money spent, the less that is experienced." The application of this law to my automobile refurbishing guaranteed lots of experience. Everything on the vehicle, except the transmission, had to be rebuilt. Luckily, the engine compression was adequate, with new piston rings, and the big end bearings were good when shimmed out with silver foil cigarette wrapping paper. From discarded Hawker Hurricane brake shoes, I removed the liners, and though the shoe diameters were different, I was able, with some astute hand filing, to replace the worn brake pads. Of course, I did not lack for advice and help from my comrades, and they participated in the exhilaration of taking our re-creation on the road. My good friend, Desi McLaughlin owned a gas station in town, and was a source of discarded parts, such as patchable tubes, spark plugs, and so on. Those were the days before self-sealing tires, so inner tubes were needed.

The car was a 1939 model Sunbeam Talbot, and quite stylish for that time. It was graced with a long, rakish bonnet (hood), nine-inch headlamps, and aerodynamic styling. With continued nurturing, it served well for five years, being an elemental factor in family and fraternal outings. When it came time for my discharge from the Army Air Corps, I had the satisfaction of giving it to a grateful comrade who was then a civilian, married, and struggling to make ends meet.

The Air Corps, being largely self-sufficient, had a very wide range of training and experience for technicians. After our initial training, our work was specialized as an airframe mechanic —that is "rigger"—, power plant mechanic, or other specialist technician, such as electrical, avionics, and so on. Given my experience before enlistment, I was naturally, assigned to the Electrical Shop.

After the Air Corps received the Percival Provosts, we witnessed the most poignant incident of my time in the Corps. The Provost was a trainer aircraft with two seats side by side. On January 3, 1957, Lieutenant Michael Flynn, a trainee pilot, was scheduled to take Provost number 182 to practice cross-country navigation. He invited my comrade Airman Jimmy Breslin, to accompany him for a fun ride. Jimmy had worked with me in a repair shop and only recently had been assigned to the flight line of Flight A. Flynn chose to navigate to his home territory in the town of Fermoy in County Cork, where his parents lived in town. It was understood that the new pilots were permitted to "show the flag" in their home town.

Having dipped his wings to his home, he attempted some maneuver that failed. He lost control of the aircraft, and plunged into a field a short distance away, east of Richmond Hill. Both flyers were killed while his family looked on. It is rumored that his mother was a nurse and that she hurried to the crash site, but when we inspected the components at Baldonnel Aerodrome that were recovered by the Army Air Corps, we calculated from the blood-stained parts and bone fragments that maternal or medical help would have been ineffective.

Much of my work was routine, but I recall an incident in that same year, in February 1957, that caused me considerable anxiety. I was at lunch in the NCO Mess when Sergeant Johnnie Mangan buttonholed me. "Dominic can you come right away and take care of a problem?" Johnnie was the most conscientious man I have ever known, and he was obviously working through lunch to clear some difficulty. Naturally, I went with him even though Flight B was strictly speaking not *my* problem. When we arrived at the hanger I saw that he was completing work on the undercarriage of a Spitfire, and he needed me to adjust the electrical system and confirm the proper operation of the "undercarriage down and locked indicator." After we were satisfied with the functioning, I "signed off" on it. I then departed to coax a late lunch from the Mess cook, while Johnnie moved the aircraft to the flight line.

While I was still relaxing at the NCO Mess, a breathless Johnnie arrived; the Spitfire had crashed while attempting to land, and there was no word on whether the pilot, Lieutenant O'Callaghan, survived. We rushed to the crash site on the runway, and saw that the aircraft fuselage was intact but upside-down, resting on its canopy. Luckily, there had not been a fire, but a fire engine stood guard amid gasoline fumes. The ambulance had departed the scene. We questioned the firemen, but all they could tell us was that the crew chief had, axed the canopy open, cut the pilot loose, and departed for the hospital. We anxiously noted that the undercarriage, now pointing skyward, appeared to be in the "down and locked" position.

Further information would have to await the hospital report and the accident investigation. In a few days everyone celebrated; the pilot's injuries were not life-threatening, even though the aircraft had to be "written off." Later, Johnnie and I were relieved to learn that the cause of the accident was an abrupt increase of engine power without the application of flight controls to counter the increased propeller torque. As the powerful 1200-horsepower Rolls Royce Merlin engine spun the propeller faster, the reactionary force on the aircraft simply caused it to counter rotate and execute a roll not prevented by sufficient aileron control.

With the energy and enthusiasm of youth, we came to some knowledge of all the technical areas in the repair shops. As well as that, we had a curiosity about aircraft in general. There was a "graveyard" for German and Allied aircraft that had crashed in Ireland during World War Two, and had been retrieved by the Army Air Corps. We followed with interest as military aviation moved to jets and helicopters, and airline aviation moved from the ubiquitous Douglas DC3's to larger aircraft and turboprops. We paid more than passing attention to the trials and failures of the emerging jetliners. Staying abreast of the broader world of aviation engineering in general was *de rigueur*. We accepted that aviation *naturally* was somewhat hazardous and read with interest the accounts of *accidents* worldwide. One disaster, in particular, affected our thinking.

In 1954, there had been a worldwide average of one air disaster per month when KLM flight 633 departed Shannon airport at 02:43 hours on September 5th for a flight to New York. Within two minutes the Lockheed Super Constellation ended in a "controlled flight into terrain" (CFIT). Of these two minutes, there was only about thirty seconds of abnormal flight encountered, that is, descending, instead of climbing.

To understand how this happened it must be taken into account that: the undercarriage, two main wheels and the nose wheel are retracted after takeoff into nacelles, to make the aircraft more aerodynamic for flight, and that the wings have extensions, called flaps, that when lowered at slow speeds, increases the lift of the wings. The undercarriage is raised and lowered by hydraulic actuators controlled by a simple lever with three positions: up, down, and neutral, for when the undercarriage is safely locked up or down, and no hydraulic action is needed. When safely locked down, the undercarriage indicator shows three green lights for the main and nose wheels. Obviously the need for "three greens" is seared into the mind of any pilot about to land. A red warning light is lit if "up" or "down" is selected and the wheels are not fully locked into position.

The only truly accidental occurrence on this flight was that *the filament of the red lamp burned out*. The pilot, unaware that the undercarriage was not retracted into the nacelles, configured the aircraft for climb by reducing the engine power and raising the flaps, thus allowing the "less-aerodynamic" aircraft in that lethal thirty seconds to descend onto the mud flats of the Shannon River. The aircraft was partially submerged, and the navigator, Johan Tieman, swam ashore, and stumbled, mud-caked, two and one-half hours later into the airport shouting, "We've crashed!" At about 07:00 hours, a rescue launch arrived at the scene to find twenty-seven persons huddled on a muddy flat. The cabin crew and twenty-five passengers inside the hull, immobilized by gasoline fumes, had drowned because of the rising tide.

We were to become very intimate with the details if this disaster because it was a concern of *Irish* aviation, got huge headlines, and the Government took a long time to thoroughly investigate it. Importantly, it provided a salutary lesson on how we should approach our work in aviation. The question we deliberated ardently was, "did the airliner fall from the sky because the lamp filament burned out?" In one sense we had to say, "yes." But even with our cursory knowledge, we could see that the deaths of twenty-eight persons, the trauma for twenty-eight survivors, and the loss of the aircraft hull need not have depended on the filament of the red lamp. The navigator performed beyond expectations, but in a different scenario, designers of the warning system, maintenance engineers, airline survival trainers, the pilots, cabin staff, air traffic control (ATC), and rescue services, all these, might have prevented the disaster. To us aspiring airmen, a job well done in aviation implied, first, a performance at a level beyond the ordinary, and second, a vigilance for circumstances beyond routine.

Engineering was absorbing, but we were, of course, also interested in taking to the skies. Despite giving us the military rank of *Airman*, the Army Air Corps had no interest in our being *thrilled* by aviation. So, it happened to be at an airfield in Lucan, County Dublin, that I had my first flying experience; there an enterprising aviation enthusiast offered air rides for a small sum that fitted my budget. The whole operation had the ethos of an air show from earlier times. First, the ride was not to go someplace but solely to experience being airborne. Second, the vehicle was an old de Havilland twin-engine, fixed-propeller, biplane, whose construction was only one technical generation from the Wright Flyer. I looked at it with, by then, a professionally jaundiced eye: were the engine cowling clips in the home-and-locked position? The fabric exterior needed touch up! From my seat I could see to the outside through ill fitting panels.

The takeoff run was short. Just as the crowds in those early flying shows in the 1920s had issued a cheer when they saw the wheels leave the grass, I felt that same elation as I became aware that we were airborne and had *broken the bond of gravity*. This was the high point of the thirty-minute trip. Theory shows that a cambered wing will produce lift when moved with speed through the air, but to experience the ordinary, commonplace wood and fabric structure lifting the machine off the ground—into another dimension—was thrilling. As the ground fell away, and the sensation of speed was lost, we appeared to be floating above a countryside so green as to be luminous; at will, one could be an observer at a crossroads or in a shopping center.

My next experience of being airborne was very different. It came about in this way. When I was put in charge of the electrical shop at Gormanston Camp, I found a number of things that needed attention. One such problem was the proper certification of aircraft batteries. Unlike what is acceptable with an automobile, an aircraft battery is subject to tests at intervals and is withdrawn from service when its capacity is less than eighty percent. I needed equipment to do this testing and spoke to my commanding officer. Captain Crehan was a pilot officer revered for his daring aerobatics. At our annual air show his loop from the runway was watched with bated breath. His attention to technical matters seemed to have been less. I had reminded him a couple of times of our needs when I learned that our cadet pilots were to begin night flying. A bad battery could lead to a complete electrical failure which, under those circumstances, would be serious. I sought him out at the Officers Mess.

"Sir I can't certify those aircraft for night flying."

"Why not?"

"I don't have the equipment to test the batteries"

Turning on his heel he barked, "You get those aircraft out. That's an order!"

I shouted toward his back, "I'm not going to lie!"

That was just the beginning of quite an uproar. The camp commander, Commandant Swan, had the captain fly me to Baldonnel the next day to get what was needed.

That flight was to be my next airborne experience. I climbed into the rear cockpit of the Chipmunk trainer, wearing a parachute, and strapped in. We took off. I cannot say if there was any malevolence in the captain's mind, but I am betting we did every maneuver in the book—loop, roll off the top, falling leaf—and maybe some that were not in the book! I was completely disoriented:, the solid green ground took off and floated eerily around and above me, strange forces were pulling my head and stomach and arms. I stretched out my arms and grasped the canopy rails at each side to keep my hands from flailing about. Although I taught a course to cadets on the theory of the basic flying instruments in front of me—the airspeed indicator, artificial horizon, altimeter, rate-of-climb, turn-and-slip, heading indicator, and vertical speed indicator—they conveyed no information I was capable of processing. At last, in the confusion, for just a moment, I spied the horizon in its proper place—ahead and beneath me. After that, I was able to grasp a little better the motions we were executing. Next, I was aware that we were in level flight, and landing at Baldonnel.

I collected the equipment needed, and after lunch was flown back to Gormanstown. The return journey was sedate enough to rival an airline flight; by which I took it, that Captain Crehan was prepared to let bygones be bygones.

This story had a good ending. Years later, when I was being discharged (technically this was being transferred to the Reserve) from the Army Air Corps, it happened that Commandant Swan was again my commanding officer. The discharge papers had a box for a "Testimonial" into which the Commandant crowded an extended description. *The Swan song* of my achievements as a technician and instructor ended with, "his character as a soldier and a man is excellent."

CHAPTER SIX

INNOVATION

My service in the Irish Army Air Corps guaranteed I would continue to be involved in the revolution that was taking place in aviation. The continuing revolution in the 1950s, motivated by the natural excitement and dreams of human aviation, made possible by peace and freedom in society, was *facilitated* by engineering innovation. My career was to be entwined with many aspects of this innovation—that at a detailed level related to arcane topics, but on a broader level, was readily understandable.

The engineering of heaver-that-air flying machines, as we have seen, began with gliders, but the rate of advance increased wildly with the success of the Wright Brothers. The first flying machines naturally relied heavily on adaptation. The Wright brothers made good use of their skills as bicycle mechanics in constructing their airplanes at Kitty Hawk! But the brothers also made ingenious and novel improvements, particularly in the design and testing of propellers, that enhanced the efficient conversion of combustion engine power to thrust. In December 1903, their devotion, research, commitment, and skill were rewarded by making the first *powered* heavier-than-air flight. In retrospect, it is simply astonishing that the Wrights mastered the *art* of controlled flight without being fatally injured, for the "wages" of innovation is inevitably increased hazards!

There were good reasons why the history of aviation from its beginning up to the 1950s, had a sense of high adventure—a hazard rate, that by any measure, was extremely unacceptable. The general public's acceptance of flying was preceded by huge fatality rates for civilian and military pilots. Such aviators warrant the descriptions of both fanatical devotion to detail and daredevil abandonment.

The statistical measures of hazard, such as fatalities per passenger mile, are rather arcane, and only descriptive in a gross way. What was important to any general acceptance of aviation was the public's sense of danger. This was even more important than both hazards and economics. In this regard, there are two important factors: first, the instinct of a thousand generations—the ingrained fear of falling: and second, the increased perception of danger through what are termed disasters, where deaths or injuries occur in multiples. Imagine, for a moment, if at the present time there were more frequent airliner incidents and that the hazard rate for fatalities still remained vanishingly small with reference to motorcycles or automobiles. Undoubtedly, the public's perception of danger in air travel would be that this was intolerable.

This perception of danger is well illustrated by the failure of the world's first airline. The loss of the German rigid airship, the Hindenburg in 1937, with a loss of thirty-two lives, spelled the end of that form of transportation. The Hindenburg had made ten trips to the Naval Air

Station (NAS) at Lakehurst New Jersey in 1936, and still its arrival on the 6 May 1937 was met by reporters and a film crew. For reasons that are still the subject of speculation, the ship caught fire during landing and was destroyed in a spectacular holocaust that consumed the ship in less than forty seconds. The resultant immediate heavy publicity shattered public acceptance of airships and dried up government support—not alone for passenger traffic, but also for any other viable uses for such cargo vessels.

While the fate of the Hindenburg well illustrates how the perception of danger in the popular imagination affects aviation, it should be noted that there were other significant factors in the abandonment of rigid airships. Operationally, rigid air ships were unable to fly above the weather or to easily divert from dangerous weather regimes. There was also rising competition from flying boats. However, the consequences of the *philosophy of engineering design* in their construction is not well appreciated. The fifteen years preceding the spectacular event at NAS Lakehurst was replete with catastrophic failures of every rigid airship built by American, British, French and German companies—revealing a failure in engineering systems' thinking, as well as the difficulties in pioneering design. The failures occurred even where the inert gas, helium, was used for buoyancy, instead of the feared flammable hydrogen gas. Given this history, the common idea that the American ban on the export of helium as a strategic war material was a factor in the failure of the airships is hardly plausible.

Engineering is sometimes thought of as the ultimate in reductionism—the engineer describing each sub-element mathematically and then, akin to the Cartesian method, synthesizing the sub-elements into a system. But in World War Two, with powerful forces unleashed from the brutal, horrifying necessities of war, a real-world approach was needed in aviation. A subtle change in design philosophy was needed—from identifying engineering as a form of physics, subject only to material causes. With a turn to the concepts of purposefulness, and optimization—a movement in engineering terms along the continuum from mechanism to organism—the idea of systems engineering was born. In a turn of phrase, science was replaced by management science. So, the innovations that make modern aviation and the exploration of space possible are not just discoveries like radar or satellite communications, but, in part, a systems engineering approach that led to operations research, modular construction, failure mode and reliability analysis, and so on.

Some of the advancement projects failed. One of the most interesting of the failures, and one that can still be visited, is the "Spruce Goose" on display at the Aviation & Space Museum in McMinnville, Oregon. A tour of this craft is a step into the history of engineering design.

In 1942, the U.S. identified a need for a large cargo aircraft to transport men and war matériel to Europe. The design chosen was a monstrous flying boat. It was to be built mostly of wood to conserve strategic materials—giving it its nickname. The grand concept exceeded 218 feet in length, 320 feet wingspan, and was powered by eight Pratt & Whitney Wasp R-4360, 2500-horsepower, engines—radial engines with twenty-eight cylinders in four rows of seven. The design specifications demanded a cruise speed of 250 mph, a range of 3000 miles, a service ceiling of 20,000 feet, and a cargo capacity of 150,000 pounds. The production effort was plagued by construction delays, and its completion became the nerve-racking undertaking of Howard Hughes. Finally, in November 1947 its one and only flight, with Hughes at the controls, was about one mile long at an altitude of seventy feet.

Also in 1942, with the tide of war turning in their favor, the Americans and British gave attention to postwar transport aircraft. We are probably seeing here the genesis of the social and civic energy that in the postwar period would produce the "baby boom" with its attendant educational and economic development, and a spirit of general optimism in the West.

In civil aviation, postwar innovation was first applied by the adaptation of war-time advances to passenger use. And in this, the American effort was to be highly successful in postwar piston engine civilian aircraft. The Lockheed, Boeing, and Douglas aircraft would dominate the long-haul market for a long time.

The British government's thinking, at this time, about post-war civil aviation, resulted in forming the famous Lord Brabazon Committee. In the next few years, the Committee defined aircraft types, and the Minister of Supply released funds for civil aircraft development. In 1945, with Nazi Germany defeated and the Soviet Union immersed in an ideological enclave, it can be said that a center of the Western way of life lay with the victorious nations. So, it is no surprise that passenger traffic on the North Atlantic became a kind of holy grail for the aircraft industry. It was a lake at the center of power akin to the Mediterranean at the cradle of Western civilization. When Charles Lindberg had "conquered" it in 1927 he records receiving messages from thirty-two nations worldwide lauding his achievement. Each reduction in cost, or price, or travel time could increase traffic. The Type I aircraft identified in the Brabazon report was to compete in this trans-Atlantic market. While undoubtedly its design concept was too closely built around a wealthy clientele, for reasons that are not entirely clear, it never garnered a single order from the airlines.

The Brabazon Committee had a visionary, Sir Jeffrey de Havilland. He, though a world apart from Howard Hughes, shared with him an unwavering excitement about human aviation and an unyielding determination to succeed. Hughes, nudged by a striving for perfection amid the complexities of innovation, faded into eccentricity, whereas de Havilland played a role in the company he founded until 1960. However, he was a tragic hero, seeing all three of his sons die in aircraft he designed, two of them as test pilots. His wife, Lois, who eagerly hand-stitched the fabric skin of his first aircraft, was crushed by the loss of her children.

De Havilland proposed a turbojet-powered airliner. While the jet engine was destined to bring major changes in the airline business, and indeed significant social changes in the world, all his fame and prestige was, at that time, needed to overcome the prevailing opinion that the aircraft would be an unattractive "fuel-hog," or worse, negating the obvious improvements in the power-to-weight ratio. In 1943, it would be very difficult to see what a really brilliant proposal this was, and the advantages in engine power, operating reliability, safety, cost, reduction in crewing needs, weather avoidance, and operating regime that it could bring.

The power-to-weight ratio of available engines was a limiting factor in aviation from the beginning. In 1929 Germany produced an *underpowered* flying boat with *twelve* reciprocating engines. In 1938, there was an attempt by BOAC to create a composite craft of two sea planes, the lower craft to be only used to assist the upper craft when takeoff power was needed. After takeoff, the two aircraft would separate, and the upper craft proceed to its trans-Atlantic destination.

Unnoticed by passengers, a small drama occurs at each aircraft takeoff. Based on a number of factors that include the length of the runway and the loaded weight, there is a speed (V1) after which the accelerating aircraft cannot stop safely, and a higher speed (V2) at which the aircraft will climb in the event of an engine failure. The no man's land between V1 and V2 is obviously greater in a low- powered aircraft! Now, as all pilots know, excess power is desirable not only at takeoff but also in recovery from any unusual flight attitudes. The Pratt & Whitney JT9D engine that powers the Boeing 747 is about one and a half times the weight of the Pratt & Whitney Wasp R-4360 engine and propeller system that was to power the "Spruce Goose." But the JT9D had roughly a tenfold increase in thrust.

The piston engine/propeller system to produce thrust is much, much more complex than the turbojet that has no reciprocating motions, and in *concept,* a single rotating turbine/compressor core. The reliability in operation that the jet engine has actually achieved would have been be a leap of imagination in 1943. First of all, engines, like all aircraft components, are removed at intervals from the airframe and overhauled—a renewal process. This routine time between overhauls (TBO) ensures against "wear out" failures. The TBO for a jet is some 500 times greater than the TBO for those postwar piston engines. However, since it is not humanly possible to have a system that never fails, so even in well-maintained engines random failures still occur. With widespread operating experience, these random failures will be observed and a statistical measures made of them. While piston engine failures were not uncommon, random jet engine failures are classified as statistically remote.

Jetliners have a remarkable advantage in the part of the atmosphere which they normally inhabit. Piston engine aircraft cruise at about 20,000 feet altitude, while the jet aircraft climb through that flight level to cruising in stratospheric altitudes of about 36,000 feet. In the stratosphere severe turbulence is less likely, and there is no danger of wing or engine icing. Also, at the higher altitudes where the jets fly, the air is thinner and aircraft fly at nearly double the ground speed for the same aerodynamic forces at lower altitudes. This reduces travel time, crewing requirements, and fuel consumption. By way of comparison, the lumbering Hindenburg air ship needed a normal crew of forty persons for its three-day trans-Atlantic trip. On the North Atlantic routes jetliner journey times entail that a flight deck crew of three complete the flight in a single shift. Also, with travel times reduced below the magical twelve hours, many potential passengers are induced to take that trip.

Accompanying the mechanical advances in aircraft structures and engine technology, was an amazing progress in avionics and instrumentation. As noted, it is simply astonishing that the Wright brothers mastered the *art* of controlled flight without being fatally injured. The whimsical movements and attitudes assumed by a kite, or, equivalently, the Wright Flyer, required extraordinary intuitive responses.

Fortunately a new piloting-friendly technology based on *angular momentum* was being explored as the very earliest experiments in aerodynamics were being made. Daily living teaches everyone to understand *linear momentum*—a heavy weight moving at high speed resists changes, such as stopping it or changing its direction of travel. However, rotational or *angular momentum* has surprising properties. When the *axis* of a spinning heavy weight component is moved, it produces measurable reactionary forces. A gyroscopic instrument is a device with a rotating component that has very high angular momentum, and the resistance of the rotating axis in space can be used to measure pitch, roll, and yaw of an aircraft. Flying instruments using these forces made flying in cloud or at night possible for those early pilots. But even in clear air in daylight, gyroscopic instruments replaced the confusing visual clues the pilot has from observing the earth's horizon, and they are protected from the motion illusions that our human vestibular system creates. "Believe your instruments" became the watchword for pilots as the *artificial-horizon* and *turn-and-slip* became basic flying instruments, not to be replaced until the computer age.

While the development of gyroscopes seemed to reach a plateau in the 1950s, the development of avionics delivered a stream of continuous improvements. Aircraft electronics encompasses radio for navigation and sound (speech) transmission. Navigation is an ancient art, but aircraft navigation soon came to depend on radio beacons rather than physical objects. The developments used various aspects of radio signals— frequency, modulation, direction of broadcast, and speed of travel of radio waves—to compute location. Some signals travel in "line-of-sight" and these are used for ADF, VOR, and DME. Due to the curvature of the Earth they are confined to be used only over relatively short distances. Lower-frequency signals follow the curvature of the Earth, and these, as in LORAN and Decca, are used for long range navigation.

Radio broadcasts modulated to carry sound (human language) had a number of challenges. Reception was often poor. The channels easily became crowded, for example, when many pilots were arriving at an airport. Furthermore, flying is, in the first place, an international activity and pilots and air traffic controllers often have different languages and accents. So, communications needed brevity, clarity, and, for want of a better word, self-evidentness. For these reasons, the use of the Morse code, prosigns, the Q code, and the phonetic alphabet were universally adopted. The dah's and dit's sounds in the headphones are pretty unmistakable as Morse code dashes and dots. Pilots universally became familiar with the Q codes and aviation's brand of the phonetic alphabet.

Imagine tuning in a radio beacon, and the headphones said dahdidit (dash, dot, dot) diditdah (dot, dot, dash) dahdididit (dash, dot, dot, dot); from your Morse code chart, this is clearly beacon DUB. But, imagine your headphones said dididit (dot, dot, dot) dahdahdah (dash, dash, dash) dididit (dot, dot, dot) you should not think just "S" "O" "S," but you should think that this is the *prosign* for the international distress signal.

The Q code is simply a three-letter code beginning with the letter "Q." It is shorthand for specific data. For example, when a pilot asks ATC for a QFE, he wants the field elevation, specifically the barometric pressure at the landing airport measured in millibars. Then he can set his altimeter so that it will read zero elevation at touchdown. Finally, the phonetic alphabet is an agreed-name for each letter. For example, imagine an aircraft with a call sign KMX, when the pilot, no matter what his native language or accent, calls out, "Kilo, Mike, X-ray," KMX would be clear to anyone familiar with the phonetic alphabet.

CHAPTER SEVEN

THE JETLINER

From the jetliner's operational advantages sprung a number of profound social effects that were hidden from the wartime planners. The initial plans envisioned an extremely wealthy clientele, whereas the North Atlantic route, for example, quickly became predominantly peopled by "ordinary folk" who could, in effect, add ten days to their vacation by flying instead of taking to the sea. The jetliner simply obliterated time, and reduced the gulf between countries and rival cultures.

There were, of course, in those days, those who were interested in conspicuous consumption and an ostentatious display of wealth. They found "jetting" from one exotic location to another to be fulfilling. They were known as the "jet set," who were attended by another new phenomenon, the aptly named "paparazzi." However, the new shrunken world was no longer exotica when businessmen, family vacationers, and tourists crowded the planes. International business prospered when a single day's travel was all that was needed to bring executives and engineers, albeit suffering some jetlag, together with their counterparts across an ocean.

The relative cost of air travel no doubt played a part in an amusing story recounted to me by a BOAC stewardess. The story goes like this: On a flight in central Africa they had picked up passengers who were on their first aircraft flight. After they reached cruise altitude her attention was drawn to a commotion in the aisle. There she found passengers were attempting to light a paraffin stove for their lunchtime repast. Obviously in this case, these particular passengers were not part of the "jet set."

The jetliners were a force for cost containment. Two factors, maintenance and crewing alone, pinpoint their potential. The phenomenal reliability and simplicity of the jet engine, reflected in the TBO, cut maintenance work. Crew salaries and training are a large part of direct airline costs. Comparing the crewing of jetliners to slower piston engine aircraft on long-haul routes, we find crew fatigue regulations demanded a second crew, with on-board sleeping quarters, for safe operation on the slower flights.

The jetliner was the stealth tool for the fashioning of globalization. Not only was the world shrunken for business travel and tourists, but also the freight capacity in frequent flights made components and goods from distant lands more readily available. This fostered the growing trend toward globalization, eroding the loyalty of corporations to their national identity and tending to reduce workers' careers to mere financial transactions. On the one hand, through increased travel, there is intimate commerce between people of different faiths and ideas, providing awareness of the manifold ways for human cooperation. On the other hand, many of these new workers labor in a dehumanized workplace, working as they do in an ecumene that is neither a country, state nor empire and separated from their cultural inheritance, social institutions, and beneficial family influences. Globalization and technology know nothing of natural law or civics and cannot satisfy the quest for human happiness. So, there is a question of whether the present increasingly technocratic society can transform itself to provide for social order, economic distribution, and civic and cultural expectations of a citizenry of democratic societies.

The story of the development of the series of Comet aircraft shows the problems that innovative front runners must bear. The de Havilland company began design work in February 1946, and a settled design was planned for delivery in 1952. Beside the turbojet engines, there were many other new, untried, design elements. First, the fuselage, the main passenger cabin, had to be engineered to be raised to a high air pressure—eight pounds per square inch higher than the ambient pressure because of flying at stratospheric altitudes. This was needed to maintain a breathable atmosphere. Beyond this challenge, the designers opted for hydraulically operated flight controls and advanced avionics (electronic navigation and communications equipment). Conscious of the need to prove the many new elements, extensive testing of all components was the order of the day. This was done by building "rigs" that tested components to the point of destruction.

In May 1952, the world's first jetliner, a BOAC Comet 1, loaded with passengers, triumphantly roared into the air from London Airport (now Heathrow), powered by four de Havilland Ghost engines, generating a total of 20,000 pounds of thrust. The Press announced the event. Pictures of its beautiful, eye-catching, streamlined form, in takeoff regime and about to claim its place in the stratosphere, were distributed worldwide. Anglophiles, and indeed aviation enthusiasts everywhere, felt a stab of pride.

But within a year the Comet 1's, in a stunning reversal, suffered three accidents during take-off, two with fatalities. It would seem that pilot error and the new hydraulic flight controls were factors in these incidents. But worse was to come! In 1954, two Comet 1's broke up in mid-air, with a loss of all lives on board. With the structural failures at altitude came explosive decompression. This, like the overpressure from a bomb, probably caused instant death as the passenger's air-filled organs—lungs, ears, and stomachs—exploded. As the fuel-laden aircraft fell into the Mediterranean they caught fire.

The first breakup involved the third aircraft off the production line and occurred about twenty minutes after takeoff from Rome. The second, eerily similar, incident involved an early production aircraft that fell into the Mediterranean, also after takeoff from Rome. These calamitous incidents caused the Comet 1's Certificate of Airworthiness to be withdrawn.

The British public was stunned! They saw national interests, British pride, and prosperity threatened. Orders for the aircraft from British, Japanese, Venezuelan, American, and Brazilian airlines were canceled. The World's imagination was horrified by accounts of men women and children being thrust into the inhospitable stratosphere and plunging 30,000 feet into the Mediterranean Sea. The prime minister, Winston Churchill, ordered up all possible resources. The Italian fishing fleet made unstinting efforts to find and retrieve flotsam, and the full might of the British Navy was turned to the recovery efforts from the depths of the sea.

A tremendous effort to investigate and redesign the jetliner sprang into action. A huge water tank was built at Farnborough, into which a complete fuselage could be immersed. Because water, unlike air, is an incompressible fluid, years of pressurization cycles were simulated quickly and safely. Using such revolutionary testing methods, a board of inquiry determined that the fuselage was subject to catastrophic failure through metal fatigue sometime after 1000 pressurization/ depressurization cycles (that is takeoff and landing cycles). This set in motion unlimited efforts to weed out any design flaws, including the building of Comet 2 and Comet 3 aircraft to prove their airworthiness. These latter were flown by the RAF. When I later joined BOAC, I heard grumblings about construction flaws as well as the design flaws. One of these included the unthinkable need for the flight engineer to carry spare cans of hydraulic fluid on board to top off reservoirs during Comet 1 flights. Remember, on this aircraft the very flight controls were hydraulically operated!

The thoroughgoing investigations were, of course, very valuable to the de Havilland team, but on a larger scale, they were salutary worldwide to the aircraft industry then engaged in a fierce, all-out international competition. Some companies increased skin thickness, some altered manufacturing methods to guard against the metal fatigue problems, and the Russians built a water tank, as the British had done at Farnborough, for fuselage testing. The crowded field for the beginning of a new jetliner era included the following aircraft: Boeing 707 and Macdonald Douglas DC8 in the United States, Sud Caravelle in France, Avro C-102 in Canada, and Tupolev TU-104 in Russia.

After the war, the Soviets lagged in jet-engine technology, but in 1946, politically left leaning English politicians, were willing to provide them the technical information on Rolls-Royce designs. By 1955, they converted their resulting jet-engine bomber to the TU-104 airliner by building onto it a fuselage that seated fifty passengers. A measure of the intensity of the East-West competition can be seen in that the Soviets flew a flight of *three* of these aircraft to London with diplomats in 1956. This jetliner saw service with Aeroflot, Czechoslovak Airlines, and the Soviet military. It retained features of its bomber heritage, such as two drogue parachutes for braking and the glassed nosecone bombardier station—in this case used for the navigator crewman.

In Canada, Avro was interested in developing a jetliner using Roll-Royce engines. In April 1950 they had built a four-engine jetliner, the C-102, that they demonstrated with air mail, but no passengers, delivered from Toronto to New York. However, various business considerations prevented further development of the C-102.

Boeing faced formidable competitors at home, as well as abroad. Their competitive edge was to be their visionary view of the *final purpose* of a jetliner. Going beyond the technical and engineering challenges they gave unstinting efforts to meet passenger and airline needs. They twice made massive redesigns of the fuselage to create superior passenger layouts. When BOAC was considering the addition of 707's to their fleet, Boeing added a large strake to the rear of the airplane to satisfy BOAC's chief pilot's desire for more lateral stability. This business orientation played a large part in the success of the 707 jetliner. The 707 was the major force in quickly converting air travel from piston engine and turboprop aircraft to jetliners.

There was also a fortuitous element, in that Boeing was in a good position to replace its in-flight refueling tanker aircraft, which at that time, was a development of the B-29 bomber. This, piston-engine aircraft, was mismatched in speed and altitude with the jet bombers it serviced. The Boeing company invested $20,000,000 of its own money to create a prototype, the Dash 80. This was a basis for both the KC-135 jet powered tanker and the 707 jetliner, with the latter, as noted, playing the pivotal role in the aviation revolution.

The culmination of the British jetliner efforts was the introduction of BOAC's Comet 4 in 1958. Although closely followed into service by the Pan Am Boeing 707, it had the pride of being the first commercial jet to cross the North Atlantic. The Comet 4 proved to be successful. The advantages in engine power, operating reliability, safety, weather avoidance, and operating regime accrued to the aircraft in which I was fortunate to be a flight crew member from 1959. This question naturally arises: why an aircraft that was the subject of catastrophic failures more renowned than the Hindenburg holocaust, and that additionally was reengineered so completely, retained the name Comet? Indeed, the French jetliner Caravelle, based in large part on the de Havilland Comet systems design, even using under license the iconic nose and cockpit design, had a much-longer commercial life. With the Comet, that visionary of aircraft design, Sir Geoffrey de Havilland, may have subordinated commercial calculations to pride and an unyielding determination to succeed.

There were, of course, other factors in the market place success, or lack thereof, of the Comet 4 beyond an airline purchasing executive's concern for the public's perception of danger. Most importantly, at its inception under the Brabazon Committee the Comet was visualized and designed as a regional airliner, not intended for long-haul Atlantic routes. To increase the routes it could fly the BOAC version was fitted with external pod fuel tanks to extend its range. But still, in those all-important transatlantic routes where the Earth's rotation forms the "jet stream" (a strong head wind to westbound high-altitude flights), the Comet 4 could not routinely fly non-stop London to New York. Direct flights (one stop), besides being less desirable for passengers, require more time, labor, fuel, and landing fees than non-stop flights.

Also, the Comet 4's configuration of engines buried in the wings could not accommodate the later more-efficient, large-diameter turbofan engines. Innovation in engine technology was such that fuel consumption per passenger mile was to become one-third of that of the first jetliners. Fuel is a major cost category, on par with labor costs, and an airline cannot compete in a market segment unless its fuel consumption is competitive.

CHAPTER EIGHT

AN EVOLVING CIVIL AVIATION

At the end of my tour of duty with the Irish Army Air Corps, I eagerly looked forward to leaving behind my meager military pay, and enjoying the salaries possible as a civilian. In 1958, I searched the advertisements in aviation magazines and soon obtained an invitation for an interview from Marshall of Cambridge, a venerable aircraft engineering company.

Clutching my various papers that attested to my technical competence and my "Swan song" discharge papers, I journeyed, by way of London, to their Cambridge facility. That provided an opportunity to meet with Frank Desmond again, and reminisce about, among other things, our "service cable crimes." He had left the service before I did, married, and now worked for BOAC at London Airport (Heathrow). As he and I, and his wife, Mairead, talked on and on, it was creeping toward midnight when I searched the newspaper for lodgings for the night. Cost was the primary consideration, so I picked the cheapest bed-and-breakfast near Paddington station, the terminus of my train into London. I phoned for a reservation, and Frank walked with me to the train station. By about 12:30 a.m. I found the establishment. After the agreed-upon price was handed over, I was directed to a room with three beds. I was quite apprehensive and decided my best strategy for defense was to lie fully clothed under a blanket. This I did, clutching my wallet in my right hand under the pillow. It had been a long day since my departure by boat from Dublin, so I drifted into an uneasy sleep. An hour or so later, I was awakened by the light being switched on. Three young men with strong Irish accents, slurred speech laced with swearing and curse words, loudly discussed what they might do. They decided they were not staying and I drifted back to sleep. The morning was a surprise. Despite the fact that the house had already secured its payment, the friendly staff produced a splendid breakfast of bacon, eggs, black pudding, potatoes, and tea and toast.

I had, in fact, many friends in London; friends not in the Aristotelian sense of virtuous friendship, nor again as mere acquaintances, but in the camaraderie of men who served a purpose together and have a treasure of common memories. It seemed the Army Air Corps training and ethos worked well in the job market. My friend, Aiden McNamara, told me how that ethos served in his particular case. He found employment as an electrician for London Underground, a far cry from the aircraft electrical systems he was used to. Aiden was determined to master the *new* technology and requested access to the blueprints. But, as a member of the junior staff, he was expected to troubleshoot failures by simple voltage testing or seeing or smelling "fried" (burnt-out) components. He had to take his case up several levels of management before he was granted free access to, what, in those days, were, the sacrosanct drawings filing cabinets.

I remember my interview with Marshall as a matter of filling out forms. A rapidly growing aviation sector needed workers, and my Irish Army Air Corps training was acceptable. In the hanger, where I worked, was another Army Air Corps friend, Bill Carroll. In that hanger, there was a great variety of projects from Douglas DC3's being refurbished for Saudi oilmen to RAF Valiant bombers being modified. I worked at Marshall a short time and was introduced to the idea of an Irishman as a "character." None of these aircraft left the hanger without the "blessing" of Paddy (who spoke with an accent *I had difficulty* understanding), who did the final cleaning. In him rested implicit trust that no screw, washer, pigtail, or other foreign object would be left in the fold of a longeron (a fore-to-aft structural member) or bulkhead.

Cambridge was an endlessly interesting city, and in the little spare time I had available I explored it. I lived at 63 Keynes Road with a nice young couple, where the lady of the house supplemented their income by taking in lodgers. I greatly admired their good, but frugal service. On Sundays, Bill and I went to Catholic Mass, where the liturgy was performed with a flourish that I deemed to be competitive with the Anglican High Church's emphasis on ritual. On some weeknights, we made friends with our English workmates by "downing a pint" at that English institution, the pub. We discovered our Irishness was not just distinguished by our accents, but by culture; our thinking was different on many issues. On one occasion, when we discussed national events, one English friend dismissed them with, "that is *their* problem." This was a quite sensible comment that the political elite would determine the outcomes, but to an Irishman, it was heresy and reeked of a class-conscious society.

From the same aviation magazines, I next found work and better pay as a flight line electrician for Cambrian Airways, a small airline that operated a fleet of Douglas DC3s and de Havilland Doves from Rhoose Airport near Cardiff. Again, I obtained lodgings, this time with a motherly old lady at 189 Barry Road in Cardiff, whose only income, I suspect, beyond her pension, was the lodger. At work, I made a *connection* with the chief engineer, who enlisted me to work on his pet project. He was rebuilding a completely disassembled de Havilland Rapide, a prewar eight-seat twin-engine passenger biplane. I mean, *completely disassembled!* In his workshop I was surprised to see the bare bones wooden wing beams. After I had moved to BOAC employment, I was delighted to read in the papers about this aircraft's "maiden" voyage.

Being new to the flight line crew, I chatted easily with the stewardesses preparing the aircraft. With one glamorous young woman we got beyond the pleasantries to her curiosity about me—who I was and where I came from. Irish! she exclaimed, without a hint of malice, "but aren't they *priest* ridden?" This exchange, and others less absolute, were influential in my thinking about religion in the daily life of my new associates.

On my days off, the bookstores in Cardiff yielded enlightenment and challenges. As expected, the Penguin edition of *The Problem of Evil* by a Church of England cleric left questions, while, *Barchester Towers* by Anthony Trollope left me confused. Trollope satirizes the very creaturely struggles in a Church of England diocese that had a weak-willed bishop with an overbearing wife. The politics are set in the struggle between the Oxford Movement and the Evangelical factions. Beyond the bishop and his wife, the characters who populate the novel are remarkably motivated by mundane things.

I was attuned to the Irish traditions, where there was still a coconsciousness of the Penal Laws and the persecution of the Church. Before television became ubiquitous, folklore in South Tipperary might turn to the gruesome death, the hanging, drawing and quartering of the martyr Father Nicholas Sheehy two hundred years earlier. The authorities had left his severed head for many years on a spike above the jail gate in Clonmel, in the foolish notion that it would repress agrarian unrest.

In the Irish milieu, both the State and Church were ordained by Providence, but, obviously, administered by humans. The contemporary clergy were, of course, treated as professionals, that is, with respect and subject to covert humorous or ill-tempered criticism. However, in theory, at least, we saw the transcendent church, enlivened by The Holy Spirit, and promised to last to the end of the age, as apart from all contemporary lay or clerical conduct. Trollope's work was funny, appealing, and commonsensical, but its lack of dealing with the transcendental aspect of his subject left me confused and questioning.

CHAPTER NINE

FLIGHT ENGINEERING

I n May 1958, I replied to a BOAC advertisement for flight engineers. A widespread notion of what flight crew do is strongly related to what a pilot does in aerial combat. Undoubtedly, that kind of flying—skilled, intuitive, "seat of the pants," daring—is at the heart of the love affair that many pilots have with their work. The *joie de vivre* is evident in Charles Lindbergh's description of a landing in his barnstorming days: "I dive down below the treetops and chandelle [a climbing turning maneuver] up around the field, climbing steeply until trembling wings warn me to level off. Then engine throttled, I sideslip down to a landing, almost brushing through high branches....[7]"

But a modern aircraft is an engineering marvel, and numerous systems for attitude control, fuel management, hydraulic actuation, cabin pressurization, climate control, navigation, warning systems, de-icing, engine operation, and so on must be managed and monitored with a myriad of controls and instruments. For aficionados of history, we note here that race cars at the turn of the century carried "flight" engineers for active technical management during a race, while the driver concentrated on "piloting." We see here also a conceptual framework inherited from naval steam-ship practice where the captain telegraphed his desire for power and a knowledgeable engine room crew maintained the various systems to deliver it as requested.

In the era of the lighter-than-air ship, more than half of the Hindenburg's normal crew of forty were flight engineers. The vital role of the flight engineer in the Yankee Clipper is highlighted by the fact that if a propeller in a Boeing B-314 was feathered, the flight engineer could crawl through a narrow passage in the wing to work on the engine in the maelstrom of flight.

In the 1950s the flying and the management of aircraft systems required three crewmen: captain, first officer, and the person variously called flight engineer, engineer officer, and second officer. The busy cockpit of those days also, depending on the route flown, needed a navigator and radio operator, as well—a total of five crewmen. It was not clear at that time, that automation and information technology would eventually eliminate the need for the engineer officer at the controls. In 1958, BOAC had just tried to fly their latest aircraft, the Bristol Britannia, with a two-man crew. After the introduction of the aircraft into service, they had been forced to retrofit them and put in a flight engineer's station. Beside the operational aspect of flying an aircraft, the engineer officer supplied another kind of valuable input: When any of the many systems malfunctioned, he was a primary source for the diagnosis and strategy for dealing with the difficulty.

Flight deck crews require two kinds of close cooperation: formal and informal. The formal cooperation is incorporated into SOPs.

Airline crews, just like medical surgeons, expect to work with tested and approved SOPs. These are reinforced by checklists to guarantee that the aircraft is properly configured for each flight regime—takeoff, climb, cruise, descent, landing, and so on. The checklist is usually called out by the non-flying pilot. Each crewmember, when responding positively gives a repeat of the check—for example, call, "booster pumps on;" positive check off of list item response, "booster pumps on"—or if things are not as they should be, "hold one." When the flight engineer calls out "full power four engines" at the beginning of the takeoff run, he is assuring the captain that *all* systems are "go" as the craft accelerates toward V1.

There also needs to be informal cooperation because when things do not go according to plan the crew must socialize and work as a unit to overcome the difficulties. The absolutely vital nature of this teamwork has been well recognized, and more recently has been known by the acronym CRM. It can best be illustrated by both an incident where it was lacking and one where it was central to saving many lives.

In December 1978, United Flight 173 departed Denver for a two-hour twenty-six-minute flight to Portland, Oregon. This flight was to be caught up in an incident that brought official recognition of a need for CRM. The flight crew—captain, first officer, and flight engineer—were all highly experienced. While on final approach to landing, they heard a loud noise and the "undercarriage down and locked" indicator failed to show the three green lights seared into the mind of pilots about to land. The captain aborted the landing. They now entered a zone where they had to prepare for an emergency landing, and their fuel consumption was high. A jet aircraft requires about five times the fuel flow for level flight at sea level over that required at cruise altitude. As the crew debated, the aircraft circled at low altitude until all four fuel-starved engines quit, and the aircraft plunged into a Portland neighborhood, killing two crew and eight passengers. The investigation found that the accident was not due to lack of knowledge, but to preoccupation with the undercarriage malfunction and the *failure of crew communications*. Moreover, the National Transportation Safety Board (NTSB) believed it to exemplify "a recurring problem of breakdown in cockpit management."

In 1979, NASA began studying cockpit crew communications in a simulator, where difficult problems could be posed and mistakes or poor strategies could be safely observed. They issued a seminal paper, and held a workshop in San Francisco where the acronym CRM was coined to apply to Cockpit Resource Management. United Airlines instituted CRM training in the early 1980s, and offered a course that was available to the airlines worldwide.

In July 1989, United Airlines Flight 232 took off from Stapleton Airport in Denver, bound for Chicago O'Hare Airport. This flight encountered problems in which CRM played a moving and spectacular role in saving lives. The aircraft was a McDonnell Douglas DC-10 which has two engines in pods underneath the wings and one buried in the tail superstructure. In route, it suffered an engine failure in the #2, tail plane, engine. This uncontained failure resulted in high-energy rotating parts being hurled out of the engine causing damage. The most consequential damage was that all three independent hydraulic systems for the operation of the aircraft's flight controls were lost. At that time, the probability of such an event was thought to be vanishingly small. On the flight deck, this had, what has been called, the "startle" effect; the pilots had difficulty in accepting that their control columns were no longer effective.

Captain Alfred C. Haynes proved to be a marvelous team leader, and, with his crew, shut down the defunct engine, and by the sole use of the throttles, righted the aircraft, which was in danger of drifting into an unrecoverable inverted attitude. As is characteristic of an aircraft without any flight controls, the aircraft began to rhythmically pitch up and down (phugoid cycle). The captain then welcomed help from a United Airlines training check captain, Dennis Fitch, who happened to be aboard. Fitch then ingeniously gained a measure of control of the aircraft by use of differential thrust of the right and left engines— possibilities never contemplated. ATC at Sioux City cleared all runways for the stricken aircraft. In a remarkable response, they gave the headings for Interstate I-29, in case the aircraft could not make the runways. As it approached for touchdown, without flaps or other flight controls to slow it down, it was traveling much too fast and with a sink rate five or six times too great. The resulting crash landing resulted in 111 of the 296 people aboard dying. Haynes later commented: "So if I hadn't used CRM, if we had not let everybody put their input in, it's a cinch we wouldn't have made it [That is no one would have survived].[8]"

On 1 September 1983 Korean Air Lines Flight 007 was shot down by Soviet forces moving the *world* closer to the un-imaginable horrors of a nuclear conflict. It presents a compelling example of inattention to detail, and likely destructive lack of CRM in the cockpit. In the Cold War era, when the superpowers were restrained by the weak logic of MAD (Mutually Assured Destruction), the 007 incident dramatically increased East/West tensions. The plane veered off course, and crossed the Kamchatka Peninsula, where Russia had secret military installations.

The Soviets ordered it shot down, and the fighter pilot can be heard praying before he releases the heat-seeking missile that sends 269 people to their death. President Reagan declared the Soviets had turned against, "the moral precepts which guide human relations," The pivotal incident appears to be the failure of the flight crew to set the proper mode of operation on the autopilot. The autopilot mode selector switch was the responsibility of both pilots, yet they failed to correct each other.

All aboard the aircraft, including both pilots, died. So, any attempt to reconstruct their failure must be speculative. It is known that in other incidents captain-to-first-officer communications in Korean Air Lines were poor, so that one can imagine the first officer deferring, instead of cross checking.

Command must be unified to be effective. There can be only one captain! In addition, the philosophy of operation inherited from World War Two highlighted the hierarchical structure and specific roles or functions for each crew member. Wartime training was organized to provide the separate skills of flying, radio communication, engineering, navigation, and so on, to meet the urgent wartime needs as quickly as was possible. In contrast, when things go wrong, such as the disastrous problems in United Flight 173, the need for *interaction* becomes paramount.

At BOAC, there was a strong emphasis on *esprit de corps* and professional interaction. But among the flight crew, only pilots could aspire to have command, creating a separate hierarchy. Flight engineers were, in fact, later encouraged to get PPL's as a hedge against flight engineering being automated out of existence, but when I worked there the World War Two ethos of separate functions was dominant. It was to be a number of years afterward when all the major airlines highlighted the crucial nature of CRM.

A particular experience I had illustrates how crew interactions worked in practice. On one occasion, at takeoff from London, the captain and first officer had attended the pre-flight briefing and had established the nature of their rapport in discussions of fuel, NOTAMS and so on. I completed my external pre-flight check, and the crew met on the flight deck. The taxi, takeoff, and initial climb out were filled with the busy attention to SOP's—formal communications. As we climbed out, the captain wished to establish the informal communications.

He switched on intercom and said, "Hi Paddy, How are things."

I replied, "My name is not Paddy."

This is followed by a long pause.

"Mr. Engineer, how are things at your station."

"Sir, things are fine here, My name is Dominic"

The captain, in being overly eager, had confused informal with familiar, but we quickly reverted to professional speech. This occasion was very much the exception. BOAC had a remarkable friendly and upbeat workplace. I remember the exceptionally fair, professional, and warm character of all my interactions there.

I took the BOAC flight engineer entrance examination. It seemed rather elementary to me, but I did not hear from them for quite some time, I was very concerned that they would decide that my Irishness could not fit into the cockpit culture. So, I wrote to inquire about the status of my application. After a further delay, I was invited for an interview. At the interview, I was amazed to see ten or more persons seated at a long table while I, nonplussed, sat at the end. It was obvious this interview had been given some policy considerations. And yes! They asked the cultural questions:

What did I do in my spare time? This was not an easy question. I did not have much spare time and the hobby I would have liked to pursue— flight training—was too expensive. However, I felt my response that "I liked to read" was well received.

What kind of books did I read? Well, I could not think of any genre of literature that I was pursuing, so I mumbled that I was reading Anthony Trollope's *Barchester Towers*. Given my conflict with Trollope's work I dreaded the next question, but I was greatly relieved that the questioner displayed no further curiosity.

Was I clear that flight engineering was not a path to being a pilot? This question/assertion could be taken as a kindly observation for my benefit. But since employees anxious for advancement generally make better employees, the concept spelled out was counter-intuitive—unless the British idea of class is included. It contained a warning not to aspire to becoming a pilot. Here were echoes of my workman friend in the Cambridge pub and his acceptance of a caste system.

It was only later on that I came to understand more fully the magnitude of the whole crew socialization problem, but at that point I sensed the question/assertion to be in some way central to my interview. I did not deem it wise, nor could I truthfully declare, I was un-ambitious. So, I said, as I honestly could, that I was interested in a technical career. The interview then seemed to end very quickly. I left very unsure of success.

BOAC's letter of acceptance that arrived shortly after the interview set off a marvelous sense of anticipation—of a career in flying, a tinge of that excitement felt with that spying of the silver machine in the County Tipperary airspace; of satisfying my ambition to travel; and of the good pay. In September of 1958, I enthusiastically joined BOAC.

CHAPTER TEN

GROUND SCHOOL
AND FLIGHT TRAINING

W hen I arrived at BOAC's huge operations center at London Airport, the cohort of trainees for flight engineer on Bristol Britannias was full. So, I spent each day in the maintenance hangers, as a sort of buddy to a kindly senior airframe mechanic. Who knows? It may have been part of an enculturation plan. Then I began the ground school to become a Comet 4 flight engineer, with about twelve or fifteen others from backgrounds in marine aviation and one from the Royal Air Force (RAF).

Many of these aspirants would not "make the cut." Some failed in mastering the breadth of knowledge. But there was another significant hurdle to success that I will label *situational awareness*—having a global viewpoint. Beyond responding to check lists and executing SOPs, or indeed even in engaging in the crucial informal communications, there was yet another characteristic that made one a vital element of the crew. I overheard a supervisor mutter "He was behind the tail plane," in other words, *he* was not functioning in the flight deck crew. Flight decks had hundreds of dials and controls for indicating and controlling the many interacting subsystems that must respond to operational demands, external conditions, and malfunctions. Intelligent responses required that crew members, even though their duties were compartmentalized, must not be preoccupied with, or fixated on, just a portion of the system, say, for example, the flight engineer's panel. Such lack of awareness leads directly to confusion when even minor things fail to happen exactly according to plan.

The group of trainees worked together, and I had the opportunity to experience the similarities and differences to my male cohort at the Irish Army Air Corps. In both groups, there were individuals who displayed surprising moral or intellectual insights, but the collective experience was different. It was clear that the English group was further along in the Western World's shift from Christianity to Secularism; the power of transcendent ideas was lessened in their lives. Their patriotism was less than the grand idea that the Irish had and it leaned more to duty. Nationalism, however, in the sense that the accident of birth was ennobling, was similar in both groups. My English group's leaning to socialism had surrendered, to a large extent, the idea of working for the common good to the bureaucracy. But it was the secularist ideas about self and sex that showed the greatest disparity. In that world there was no hereafter. This was not a dogmatic assertion, but part of their daily calculus. Death itself was not denied, but robbed of meaning; the self at death merely *passed* away. In regard to sexual mores, I found in casual chatter, not discounted for the expected bravado, that marriage was a contract, not a sacrament; that fornication and adultery were naughty, not sinful; and most amazingly the marriage act was naughty, not sacred.

They assumed that Irish equated to Catholic, and assailed Catholicism mostly because of curiosity or questioning. I found it interesting that their earnest questions rested on an underlying belief in *sola scriptura*: did Catholics forbid reading the Bible? Had they restricted access to it by chaining it to a pillar in churches? For my part, I felt in general, that they had been robbed of their birthright. The narrowing of the universe they inhabited is epitomized in a story recounted about my English grandmother: Elizabeth Mary Colvert was gravely ill and unable to attend her son's wedding. When Joe and Irene, in their wedding attire came to her bedside, she exclaimed, "I can die now that my youngest child is married!" The hereafter was very much part of *her* calculus.

None of us had apologetical or controversialist skills to address our philosophical or theological differences. I suffered their discussions of real and imagined lapses in silence unless directly challenged; I knew the schoolyard rule that, a challenge unanswered is a defeat. So, I sought a superiority in technical matters and an uneasy truce about higher things.

Terry Hardeman was from the RAF background, and so, also not well favored in the group dynamics. He illuminated these dynamics for me when he commented, "Dominic you are *free* to say what you want, but I cannot." We engaged in friendly and stimulating discussions. Terry had a great interest in the theories of L. Ron Hubbard. Of course, Hubbard claimed his system did not rest on theories, but axioms, and that Scientology was "engineered" from an apodictic base with no leap of faith needed. Although, we were both aware that the "dismal sciences" of the 1800s had based their false conclusions on indisputable mathematics, we were still very partial to the idea that knowledge was based on science and engineering, and we could find no flaw in Hubbard's presentation. Neither Terry nor I had the philosophical training to evaluate or counter the arguments in *Dianetics,* but the more fantastical claims were unbelievable in my world view.[9] Terry whose *weltanschauung* was differently formed had some hope that he had found a key to the transformation to superman—Hubbard's "clear." The Hubbardian theory suggested obtaining an objective view by out-of-body experiences. When Terry issued the command of Scientology's rubrics, "be three feet behind your head," *nothing happened.* In this way, we came to a more unified view.

Beside the class work in general aviation topics, we studied all the Comet 4 systems. In any spare time, we practiced drills on Comet 4 cockpit mockups, setting up the controls for operational and emergency situations. Great familiarity with the location of switches and dials was essential to a normal response!

I found myself greatly intrigued by the survival training manuals, which dealt with the possibility of a forced landing or a ditching at sea. The manuals were segmented into Arctic, Desert, Tropics, and Ocean. Each of these areas was the subject of an Air Ministry pamphlet or pocket book based on scientific knowledge and practical things garnered from actual experiences. For example, the tropics survival advice pictured a method for breaking open coconuts without special equipment. The back pages had appendices with those ubiquitous check lists, like the challenging sixteen-item, "Vital Actions after Boarding the Multi-seat Dinghy." Although the integration of this kind of information into our thinking required considerable mental gymnastics, it served to reinforce the concept of a planned response to chaos.

While the possibility of cataclysmic disasters had to be contemplated with dread, the commitment to heroic action was not morbid, but good.

In a disaster, one might be called upon for noble, clever, quick, brainy responses. I resolved that this would not be a challenge I would fail! We studied the use of emergency equipment carried aboard the aircraft, such as, the hand-cranked signal generators and flare guns. The manuals were based on the knowledge gleaned from the actual experiences of military situations. We studied drills for deployment and use of the dinghies (air inflatable rubber craft) in the event of ditching (landing on water). There was, of course, no way to guess what conditions would prevail after a disaster, but surviving crew members would be expected to take command of each dingy.

We had a simulated drill of exiting a burning aircraft using an old aircraft fuselage and real smoke. There it was demonstrated that the toxic fumes, being lighter than air, do not reach to the floor, and breathable air is available for a couple of inches at floor level in a cabin fire. For even more exotic situations we were dependent on our imaginations and the stories of what transpired in previous disasters. These types of stories and the ability to conduct a thought game of bizarre circumstances, are, of course, the essential elements of all disaster preparedness. Knowing what can happen is primary. Imagination, far from being deception or idleness, is the key to strategizing and dealing with the practicalities and mental stress.

Many things in our surroundings reinforced this need for mental awareness; we were told the Avro York freighter, kept ready to fly a spare engine to any point worldwide, carried a stash of Maria Theresia dollars. We knew these were the only currency that could buy influence with the murderous Arab tribes known to still be a danger to downed airmen in the Sahara Desert. There was also a sad story of a young Coastal Command airman downed in the mid-Atlantic. In this folklore, the young airman, forced from the intimate atmosphere of the cockpit to the limitless turbulent ocean surface, so the story goes, *lost the will to live*. He was dead when rescue forces lifted him from the dinghy the next day. Although we recognized this story as apocryphal it was undoubtedly based on real experiences.

We trainees also had scheduled sessions in the Comet 4 simulator. This simulator was a marvel that must have cost as much or more than an aircraft and reinforced the idea that the airline business is capital-intensive, with large, fixed costs. The interior was an exact replica of the Comet 4 cockpit and the structure was capable of limited pitch and roll. The "windscreen" depicted the take off runway. This was before the days of general-purpose digital computers, so it can only be imagined the ingenuity and effort to simulate each instrument and system for all the functions of flying and malfunctions.

In one session, we simulated the failure of all four engines and began a gliding descent. Starting a jet engine requires that it be rotating at high RPM to compress the intake air. Without compression, combustion will not take place. In flight, this is accomplished by "windmilling" the engine, in effect, flying, and in this case descending, at an airspeed of 185 knots. Adjusting the glide ratio, we achieved the required RPM and reintroduced fuel and ignition, successfully simulating the restarting procedures.

BOAC aspired to the ideals of the *senior* service, the Navy. We were issued a blue uniform. Our white shirts had purple *engineering* stripes on the epaulettes. Our hats had removable white covers for the crowns, though this idea was later abandoned. We were expected to follow the Navy practice to wear a white crown when serving in the tropics. Some say the uniform makes the man, and some say the man makes the uniform. Whichever bromide you prefer we felt ready and committed to all the demands of flight engineering.

In May 1959, we were ready to begin flying training. During June 1959, I participated in about fifteen training flights. In these flights, three aspiring flight engineers shared time operating the controls and logging progress under the watchful eye of the flight supervisors. I was *lucky* enough to be at the controls when a flight emergency arose: We were overhead Shannon Airport when a fire alarm sounded. There were no noticeable secondary effects, so we suspected an alarm malfunction, however, it was clear we should land as soon as possible.

The weight, the AUW of an aircraft, is limited for landing because of potential structural damage when a flying machine touches down with a heavy load of fuel. Note that attempting a "greaser," an imperceptible landing, may not be a solution. In particular, if there is an element of a cross wind, the aircraft while flying, must assume a heading into the wind to track in line with the runway. When it becomes necessary to convert the flying machine to a wheeled machine by aligning the heading with the tracking, it must be quickly plunked down onto the runway.

In our situation, the AUW exceeded the permissible landing weight, since we had loaded fuel enough to carry out a number of training maneuvers before landing. A decision had to be made, whether to circle while burning off sufficient weight of fuel or to jettison the fuel to reach the AUW of the 52,000 kilos permitted. A decision to jettison, or dump, as it is called, is not undertaken lightly, since the dumped fuel forms a combustible vapor between its liquid and dissipation states. In this case, I got to perform the highly unusual procedure of spraying tons of jet fuel over the Atlantic Ocean.

CHAPTER ELEVEN

NORTH ATLANTIC OPERATIONS

My first operational flight was on G-ADPL on Wednesday 1 July 1959. I arrived at the aircraft by bus from Comet 4 operations, Building 221, and completed the preflight check with thoroughness. We took off from London Airport (now Heathrow) about noon and refueled at Sydney, Nova Scotia. When these flights stopped, as they normally did, at Gander, Newfoundland, refueling would be completed in about twenty minutes. To achieve that kind of turnaround, passengers were not permitted to deplane. Due to the weather at Gander, our transit was through Sidney, and was an unusual one hour and twenty minutes. We then continued on to New York, and I arrived at Idlewild (now Kennedy) Airport about 5:30 p.m. local time, feeling a strong sense of accomplishment. Nine hours and seven minutes had elapsed since our departure from London.

In New York, BOAC crews stayed at what was then known as, the Shelton Towers Hotel, on Fifth Avenue. It is interesting to note, that BOAC boasted two names: One, on the North Atlantic routes, termed Boack, and on all other routes termed "B" "O" "A" "C." With the Boack culture, there was no crew socialization during the stay over in New York. Each crew member busied himself in the metropolis until time for duty. This fitted well with my plans. On my next trip to New York in August, I visited in the suburbs with my ex-Irish Army Air Corps friend, Tommy Keaveney. Tommy had immigrated and was living with his American cousins, who provided a wonderfully warm welcome. New York was a great experience for me and I marveled at the skyscrapers, the gigantic automobiles (in comparison to European automobiles), and the palpable energy and dynamism of the city.

In August I had a girl friend in New York. I had met Catherine in 1956, when she was part of the postwar influx of American travelers touring Europe. After her return home to San Francisco, we corresponded warmly, bridging the impossible distance with news of our activities; we had struck a genuine chord of friendship. But Providence was at work: that year, Catherine accepted a scholarship for graduate work at Columbia University in New York. Though we were definitely not "jet set," we were to be poster boy and girl for jet age courtship.

Early on Sunday, August 16, I set out from the Shelton Towers to find Catherine. My very first personal interaction was unusual in the eyes of those who see New Yorkers as curt and unhelpful. On Fifth Avenue I found the closest bus stop. There I consulted a middle aged-matron on the possible buses to Broadway and Morningside Drive. Generously, she carefully juggled routes, locations, and Sunday schedules, and then declared she would divert from her own journey to accompany me to where I must change buses. Knowing something of America's founding, and, in particular, the stories of some who had emigrated there, I was not, in fact, surprised by the warm human response.

Every love story is unique. However, the fervor, the anguish, and the ecstasy of romance that we experienced is endlessly explored in every art form. In the next year and a half, I flew to New York on duty seven times before the Comet 4 was withdrawn from that route, and I was able to use my flight crew privileges for other trips.

Catherine was studying social work in a doctoral program. At that time, sociology held the high hopes of many in the social work field for a breakthrough in understanding and improving the human condition. Sociology's mathematical approach was considered a natural evolution of the social sciences, similar to the mathematization of physics and chemistry.

In our time together in New York, our most important communications were wordless. As a healthy male, I was prepared to be overpowered by femininity alone, but when I looked in her eyes, I was stunned by her grace and spirit of innocence. We used those times to explore the mundane, as well as the philosophic—often in Johnny Johnson's steakhouse on Third Avenue. Our careers, in flying and social work and the instability of postwar world affairs, provided for plenty of chatter. The philosophic discussions revolved around Charles Frankel's *The Case for Modern Man*. This was required reading in her course work. But more than that, the liberal intellectualism of the work was pervasive of the Columbia program.[10] Frankel opens the work by railing against "The prophets who tell us that this revolution of modernity has been a failure." While some of the polemic was cavalier and not to be taken literally, he made two points repeatedly and firmly: relativism is supreme, there are no absolutes; and objectivity comes only through science (mathematics). In the concluding chapters of the work, he claims:

"However difficult these problems with which liberalism is confronted may be, they are institutional, not psychological—political not moral."

Catherine disagreed with much of it, and her marginal notes in the book are mostly negative. One just says, "despair" a sentiment directed to the lack of intellectual rigor. Frankel's dialectic simply did not engage rigorously with the nature of truth or of human existence. The rampant reductionism caused her to lose confidence in Columbia's educational process. She wondered, how could relativism be absolute if there are no absolutes? How could spiritual things like love and marriage and compassion exist if the *really real* is material, and there is no metaphysics? While her course work went extremely well, her independent mindedness and resistance to being an acolyte led her to express impolitic views. Her professor expounded that she had, "a childhood that was *too* happy."

We discussed her studies in psychoanalysis. At that time Freud was a revered guru, generally awarded Olympian status. I was awed and delighted with her open-mindedness. She looked for the objective truth of his insights and the potential to help patients or clients, balancing them against Freud's flawed personality and the limited population on which his conclusions were based. I was very much the listener, but my involvement with technology, the product of science, made me attuned to the scientific claims. At that time, the claims that Scientology, Relativism, and Psychoanalysis were hard sciences made me think that I was facing a pervasive modern confusion that confined reality to the mechanical.

Fortunately, we did not fall prey to the idea then gaining wider currency that love is intimacy—it is thought that the origin of sexual revolution, the reduction of love to the erotic, can be dated to 1959–60. We were anxious to find a transcendent meaning in our relationship, something beyond the cinematic versions we enjoyed so much. Higher, more realistic ideals of love, were a necessary part of our building toward a commitment to "until death do us part." Our election to delay the good that comes with natural passion, and to be zealous for the apt fulfillment of the *other* rather than a mere mutual exploitation, gave us an authentic freedom to struggle with doubts, personalities, schedules, time zones, cultural questions, family involvement, emigration, travel, housing, and the inbuilt differences of male and female.

In London, at 637 London Road, I lived in Hounslow, in a "bedsitter," one step up from "lodger." Catherine would become a "renter" in a charming flat at 5 Popes Grove, two blocks from the renowned Twickenham Green, and walking distance from Richmond Park with its wild deer and panoramic views. After Catherine's immigration to England in September, we busied ourselves with wedding arrangements. My pastor decided the ceremony should be in *my* parish church.

On a glorious sunny Tuesday, October 4, 1960, in Saint Vincent de Paul church in Hounslow, Middlesex, England, we exchanged vows. Events of that day transpired with a surreal quality, but I had no doubt that the "I do" affirmation was effective beyond the here and now and made a mark in *eternity*.

I was due to leave on Sunday for a thirteen-day trip that would take me to Tokyo, so there was not time for a proper, leisurely honeymoon. Under the circumstances, we promised ourselves an episodic honeymoon—short trips exploring London and the delightful surrounding counties as flying duty and finances permitted. We did spend the remainder of the week at the historic Oxford Inn, exploring that fabled city of Oxford and Shakespeare Country.

Only one of my west-bound flights made it non-stop to New York; flight 509/474, on 1 March 1960 made it in eight hours and twenty-eight minutes. That was to be the longest duration of any flight I made in a Comet 4. Due to the favorable jet stream, most Comet 4 east bound flights did make non-stop flights from New York to London, but in my case we had to divert twice to refuel at Shannon and once to Southhampton. The fuel remaining depended on whether the flight had been impeded by a headwind or advanced by a tailwind. These were important variables as the trans-Atlantic flights approached their eastern or western destinations.

Aircraft fuel is accounted for, not by volume, but by its weight, that represents its energy content. The quantities uploaded are accurately metered and converted to weight by the known kilograms per gallon. But in flight the kilograms remaining is not a simple matter of "checking the gas gauge." For instance, the fuel is stored in wing tanks that are necessarily shallow with a large area. This means that an imperceptible disparity of a fuel level reading at any point in such a tank in flight represents a very large volume of fuel. For fuel management, the rate of fuel flow to each engine was metered accurately and the fuel consumed with varying flows was calculated and recorded by the flight engineer. In addition, the flow meters had a built-in integrating function. At any time, using the flight engineers log, with its calculated flows, readings from the fuel flow integrators, and tank readings, the fuel remaining would be calculated.

As noted, an important variable was the winds aloft. These are normally estimated in a flight plan based on the experience of an aircraft that has recently flown that flight path. But the first jetliners did not have the benefit of recent traffic at those higher altitudes at which they operated. As a flight approached either side of the Atlantic, the destination airports available to it would be calculated by the availability of three quantities of fuel: 1) fuel to fly to the destination airport, 2) fuel for further flying to a viable alternate airport, and 3) fuel for sixty minutes "holding" (flying in circles). I remember the first time a captain turned to me somewhere west of Shannon as we were bound for London and asked, "what will be our fuel at so and so hours (thirty minutes later)." My first reaction was, I had better be right! On that occasion, with some consultation with the navigator, who had the flight planning data, and the knowledge that we were cleared by ATC to climb to where fuel flows would decrease, we worked out the figure. These were the kinds of problems in which we were engrossed, and nothing of the feared cultural clash raised its ugly head. There was a universal feeling that we were all on the "cutting edge" of an exciting development in aviation and society.

All the North Atlantic flights carried a navigator. Those were the days before satellite positioning (GPS) and inertial (gyroscopic) navigation were available. The Comet 4 carried a sextant that could be placed in a port in the roof of the cockpit for sighting celestial bodies. The sightings gave the bearing of the aircraft toward the selected celestial object, and usually three bearings would give an accurate position of the aircraft. Radio bearings could be taken on known ground radio stations within the range of their signals and on the weather ships *Charlie* and *Juliet* that kept station mid-Atlantic. Positioning was also possible using radio short-range navigational aids VOR and DME. The navigational aids, LORAN and Decca were used for long-range navigation. The interpretation and crosschecking of the many navigational devices provided accurate accounts of our tracking and drift, and kept a navigator quite busy.

Beyond navigation in the horizontal dimensions, assignment of the other dimensions—altitude and time—was in the hands of ATC. They typically say in giving clearance, "climb to and maintain" a particular altitude. Thus, ATC maintains a vertical separation of traffic. Now in long-haul flights, an aircraft becomes significantly lighter as it burns off fuel. The lighter aircraft could then reduce fuel consumption if it is allowed to ascend to cruise at a higher altitude. However, in the mid-Atlantic, we were out of the range of ATC and could not request a change in flight level. Unlike later times, when those slots, that is, the cruise altitudes/times spaces were crowded, in those early jetliner flights we could often be given a climb/cruise clearance. In that case, the autopilot was set to maintain an airspeed (not altitude), and the aircraft was allowed to drift higher as its weight decreased. This meant that we conserved every possible drop of that precious fuel.

After the jetliner service was established, the Comets were retrofitted with many improvements that contributed to performance and safety. Both braking capacity and the aquaplaning that occurs on wet runways caused a lot of concern. Reverse thrust may have been the most notable improvement to the Comet 4 operations. Without it, the aircraft was dependent on the heat capacity of the wheel brakes and the frictional adherence of the tires to the landing runway. Reverse thrusters assisted with both these problems. Anti-lock braking systems were at that time a new technology and were adopted by aircraft (and later as ABS for automobiles). The Comet 4 was retrofitted with Maxarets, Dunlop's anti-lock braking systems, which reduced the landing distance by reducing skidding and aquaplaning. Brake capacity continued to be a problem. One ground engineer, with responsibility for meeting aircraft, noted that the brakes could be glowing red hot on arrival at the tarmac.[11] Cooling fans were installed in the wheels to lessen that problem.

Weather radar was another reassuring improvement. At our cruising altitudes, we mostly encountered clear air or thin wispy stratus cloud. However, particularly in the tropics, storms often reach such altitudes. Weather radar literally painted a picture of the environment, thus allowing us to map our position in regard to the dangerous, dense watery cores of ice and rain of cumulonimbus storm clouds. This allowed us to select a safe course around and between those storms.

In 1958, these were the earliest jetliner flights and there was naturally considerable expectation that problems would arise. Indeed, flight crews were keenly aware that brilliant minds and the best engineering judgment had failed to foresee the catastrophic metal fatigue problem that dramatically plunged the shattered parts of two Comet 1's into the Mediterranean four years earlier.

With the Comet 4, all systems worked as planned, that is to say, with constant minor modifications and improvements, as is expected with complex machinery. We soon came to believe that we were not just graced with good luck. We *knew* we were the operators of an extremely reliable, productive, and sophisticated technical platform at the pinnacle of technical innovation, that had been built on the sacrificial daring of many. A new era of international travel was established.

Of course, the innovative engineering had, in each case, been flown by a test pilot to prove its viability or need for revision. Before a certificate of airworthiness is given, a test pilot, among a myriad of things, must test the performance of flight control surfaces, and the recovery of control from unusual attitudes. As we have noted, in the case of Sir. Jeffery de Havilland's sons, some of these test pilots paid the ultimate price. Our part required devotion and vigilance because, as we came to understand, accidents and hazardous incidents often can be traced back to pivotal events that appear trivial and innocent at first.

CHAPTER TWELVE

ADVENTURES CLOSE TO HOME

In those years, there was a series of unassuming two-story buildings, built with a wartime utilitarian mindset, at what was known as London Airport North. One of these, Building 221, housed Comet 4 Operations. BOAC's huge maintenance facility, where the aircraft were serviced, was located at a distance, from which the readied aircraft was towed to the tarmac adjacent to the passenger terminal at London Airport North. "Jetways" (passenger boarding bridges) were not to be a feature of airports for some time, so the front and rear entrances of the aircraft were then provided with open passenger boarding staircases. Passengers arrived by bus from the terminal, and the crew came by bus from Comet Operations. English weather saw to it that there was often good use for a supply of umbrellas adjacent to those open staircases. From that spot, all Comet 4 routes emanated to the "ends of the Earth": New York; Santiago, Chile; Johannesburg, South Africa; Melbourne,

Australia; Tokyo, Japan; and numerous destinations in between. The productivity of jet planes can be imagined by noting that the BOAC fleet spanning this global route structure would only grow to nineteen aircraft.

All our flight crews were based in London. With their briefcase and appropriately packed suitcase for the proposed trip they were dropped off at Building 221, or they parked their car in a nearby reserved lot. Check-in was a minimum of two hours prior to departure time. This was very strictly adhered to. Living in Hounslow and later in Twickenham that were close to Heathrow, I received a number of calls for substitution when some unfortunate event prevented a flight engineer from making that deadline.

Check-in was the beginning of a work day that was statutorily limited to sixteen hours by the CAA (British Civil Aviation Authority). The FAA (U.S. Federal Aviation Authority) had a limit of twelve-hour duty day in 1959. These regulations for flight time limitations (FTL) were made by each country to promote safety through the prevention of fatigue of flight crews. FTL continues to be an area of very active interest due to the complexity of practical considerations about the personal use of time. A particular consideration is that by necessity the end of any flight crew day has the most intense activity. Even if the end of the day comes with a standard operating procedure, as it usually does, and without complications in weather, traffic, or malfunctions, that final landing still requires full attention to both details and overarching rules, in addition to well formed intuitive judgments.

Mental energy and jet lag are fatiguing. I was to have a particular experience of this in November 1959. Due to unusual circumstances, I had a trip that began in New Delhi. To make this possible, I deadheaded (flew as a passenger) from London to New Delhi in the first week of the month. This flying as passenger required four landings and thirteen or fourteen hours in the air. Then on Sunday the 8th I was the flight engineer for a sector New Delhi to Bahrain. On Monday, we flew a short sector of three hours to Beirut. On Wednesday, the longest duty day of that trip, in about seven hours flying time we flew two sectors back to London.[12] One could say, not a very strenuous trip by our standards; but being new to the job I experienced some jet lag and expended a large amount of mental energy by the time I got home on Wednesday evening. Thursday, feeling tired, I went to bed early. I awoke in the morning refreshed, and peering out the window to check on my parked car and was puzzled to notice my car had been issued a parking ticket. The street there had a two-hour parking restriction beginning at 8 o'clock, and it was not yet 10 o'clock! It took some time before it sank in—I had slept through Friday and it was now Saturday.

Poor Mrs. Woods, my landlady got a terrible fright. Being a "bedsitter" and not a lodger she only discretely looked in my room when I was away; but as Friday had wore on she became concerned. Seeing my "lifeless" form she panicked. Guiltily she thought, "had I expired from carbon monoxide poisoning from the unvented gas fireplace." She ran for her husband to investigate. The problem had nothing to do with the fireplace, but by the time of my return from my next trip a new *vented* gas heater had been installed.

It took very little experience of the constant calls to duty to find packing for a trip extremely easy. The suitcase had the same items more or less—whether a long or short trip. The briefcase was an office at home or away from home. Although, as I note later this system broke down causing some anxious moments on a trip to Cairo when I arrived there minus the most vital document—a passport. In the briefcase, all flight engineers prided themselves with having a personalized set of hand tools which they would use in imagined emergencies. I would heartily agree that this was a figment of their imagination, a mere conceit; except I found use for mine on occasion, and in one situation averted a catastrophe.

One captain recounted a story that was good for a hearty laugh by the *cognoscente*. The story goes:

An engineer officer was captivated with the unique clamping forces exercised by that mundane item, the clothespin. He carried one in his personalized kit for many many years. On this occasion the ON/OFF switch for the autopilot failed. This switch was a knob that was pulled upward and maintained in this ON position by an electromagnet. Now with the failure of the electromagnet, the captain had the option of manually flying the aircraft or maintaining the autopilot operation ON by physically holding the knob up for several hours. However, to everyone's immense satisfaction and relief, the engineer rummaged among the debris in his briefcase and dusted off the clothespin—an almost perfect solution, and vindication of the engineer.

On one occasion, my personal tool kit provided, not a perfect solution, but a *vital* solution. I do not recall the sector now, but somewhere in the Middle East during cruise the captain smelled smoke. Very soon it was apparent it was coming from a box on a panel by the captains left leg. He gave control to the first officer, and the pilots went on oxygen. He vacated his seat, while I made a close examination of the overheating box. I looked in vain for the expected label to identify it. With the label information I could locate its circuit breaker from among the hundreds on the circuit breaker panel behind my station.

The smoke was getting worse. I consulted the operating manual, a five-hundred-page book stowed at the engineer's station. It took a minute, but I located the diagram of the panel showing the outline of the offending box, *but again there was no label to identify it.* The smoke was getting worse, and the box was too hot to touch. Now fire in the cockpit is greatly to be feared; no amount of heroism or creativity is of use if the crew are unable to exercise control. I made a quick decision, possibly the only decision now open to me; I foraged in my brief case and retrieved a wire snips, and cut all the cables from the back of the box.

After we arrived safely on the ground, we discovered the problem. The first officer had failed, despite it being a checklist item, to switch off the windshield wipers after takeoff. As the aircraft accelerated to speed, the slipstream stalled the wipers, giving the appearance that they were switched off. The wiper hydraulic pump motor had starter resistors designed for intermittent use in that box; in continuous operation these had overheated.

Email and social media was then not even a concept, international telephone rates were astronomical, and since letter writing could not be reserved to off-duty periods the briefcase held one's active correspondence. The counterpart to letter writing was that, if there had not been rescheduling during a trip and if the international postal service delivered as promised, crew members could expect to receive a letter from home at many hotels along the way. Of course, when the system failed one might get a, still welcome, letter from a previous trip. It was through this creaky system I learned of Catherine's struggles and triumphs in acculturation—a giggle at her American accent instead of the proper response from a store assistant, a balky *manual* choke control, a feature unfamiliar to Americans, on our car, and the very useful services of the milkman.

In Twickenham the milkman made his daily rounds, collecting empty milk bottles and placing milk and other products in an agreed shady spot by the door. She could depend on the milkman to bring the ingredients of the English breakfast that brought a little salve to the aching of unsullied love for the presence of the loved one when I was away, and brought a festive spirit to breakfast when I got home. In Catherine's American mind, the milkman was an exotic throw back to a dreamy domestic life. At the end of the week, placing a check for the goods with the empty bottles had more the feel of gifting a friend than a commercial transaction.

After check-in at Building 221, flight engineers reviewed the latest revisions to the aircraft operating manual before heading to the tarmac to make the preflight inspection. There was a high level of confidence that the ground crew at home base had taken proper care of everything, but this would be not be an excuse for any lack of vigilance.

In an aircraft, as in any such complex system, there were, of course, a stream of modifications and improvements. And knowing of a "mod (modification)" could be a warning to see how it behaved in practice. An example here could be the introduction of safety valves on the wheels. A heavily loaded airplane increases the length of the take-off run and increases the flexing of the tires. These conditions together with braking during taxing cause heat buildup in the wheels. After takeoff the wheels (undercarriage) are retracted into a close fitting nacelle where the residual heat could cause the temperature of the tires to reach high levels. Heated air expands increasing the tire air pressure possibly to explosive levels. As a protection the wheel hubs of the Comet 4 were fitted with valves filled with solder that would melt before a dangerous temperature/pressure was reached. When I experienced two flat tires on landing it was easy—

and reassuring—to find the culprit was the modified wheels I had read about in Building 221.

In general flight time limitations made it unlikely that our first crew stopover would be in the European cities we serviced. A non-stop flight to Beirut was about five hours flying time and a three-sector flight to Teheran was comfortably within a working day. However, two of my stopovers in Europe were particularly memorable. In July 1960, we were *forced* by aircraft problems to a stopover in Frankfurt; and in June 1962, I was scheduled for a trip which flew first to Frankfurt a then on to a delightful Roman stopover.

Flight 755 took off from Cairo for Frankfurt on the evening of the 24 July 1960. Our departure time from was 7:36 p.m. We were well into the cruise portion of the flight when I saw that the Green System (Main flight controls system) hydraulic reservoir indicator showed only seven eights full. I opened a discussion with Captain Rowe with, "we may have trouble here," and described what was happening.

I continued to monitor it for a minute and noted a further decline. The implication of this further decline is that the indication is not just an instrument error but an actual continuing loss of fluid. Engineering judgment also suggested the fault was more likely to be in the dynamic parts of the system rather than in the static piping.

As noted earlier, the Comet was the first aircraft fitted with flight controls actuated by hydraulics instead of a fully mechanical system operated by cables. A terrifying thought is: without functioning hydraulics none of the flight controls—ailerons, rudder, elevators—could be moved; the pilot would be forced to inaction while the aircraft flew to its doom. Of course, the Comet 4 had its engines buried in the wings close to the longitudinal center so that even the heroic, creative steering strategies used by Unite*d Airlines flight 232 would not work.*[13]

Now, the aircraft was designed with a complex of four flight hydraulic systems, two of which (Green and Blue) were complete duplicates. In the roof of the flight deck there were a set of crimson colored hydraulic system selection levers, never to be touched except in dire circumstances, and, of course, in practice never moved.

I proposed we move to the Blue system. But Captain Rowe was hesitant to interfere with the primary flight controls. No doubt, as good pilots do, he first thought was of the closest alternate airport. However, my thinking was, first that, the rate of fluid loss is high and second, a leaking seal on a moving actuator (in this case called a servodyne) can easily progress to a blowout instantly freezing the pilots controls. I insisted, "we must move to the Blue system," to which he nodded assent. I reached up and made the selection with both pilots carefully monitoring their instruments. There was no perceptible reaction. The Green reservoir indicator also now held steady, confirming that the servodyne was at fault, since a static pipe would have continued to leak at the same rate.

An interesting sequel to this incident occurred after we landed at Frankfurt. While I was discussing the flight controls with the station engineer, I discovered there was on board a man who was being flown to London for emergency medical treatment. Flight Operations, while they were sizing up the situation, had announced a customary *one-hour* delay. All the other passengers had exited, but the sick man's nurses decided that for an hour's wait, staying on the aircraft was best. I advised them to get to the head of the line for an alternate flight. I told them, "this aircraft will not be leaving for quite some time." It would, of course, require specialist mechanics and large replacement parts to be flown in from London to fix things. We were able to depart Frankfurt the next day, a little over twenty-four hours later.

When I learned in June of 1962 that on an upcoming trip the crew would have a stopover of about forty-eight hours in Rome, Catherine and I were still thinking of the episodic honeymoon promise we had made to ourselves. So, we got her a ticket to accompany me to Rome. Catherine had fond memories of Rome from when she visited there in 1956.

After takeoff from Frankfurt, I fetched her from the passenger cabin and seated her on the flight deck. Customarily at top-of-descent cockpit visitors were asked to return to their seats; but cordial Captain Bailey insisted she remain on the flight deck in a ring side (the radio officer's) seat, and he found her a set of headphones to listen to the landing chatter. The language for air traffic control (ATC) is an internationally agreed to set of controlled English phrases. So, armed with our call sign, "speedbird 942," she could identify the radio chatter that applied to us as we made a midnight landing at Rome's Fiumicino airport on Saturday. She long remembered what passengers never see: the bird's eye view of the approach, the strobe lightning behaving as a giant dynamic arrow encouraging the pilot onto the lighted runway. Later she exclaimed, "you could not miss."

The only downside to our mini-honeymoon was that I had a departure time for Damascus shortly after midnight on Tuesday. For convenience Catherine accompanied me on the crew transport to pick up her return flight to London, that was to come through much later in the morning. The almost deserted airport had an eerie feeling. She was more than pleased, indeed greatly relieved, when the flight desk opened up for her return flight.

Otherwise everything worked for the best. At the hotel, I was a crew member unexpectedly arriving with a wife—Roman hospitality handled it seamlessly and we were assigned a splendid room, I thought later the honeymoon suite, without any questions been asked. I do not remember now if there was an additional charge.

The Quirnale Hotel where we stayed, was itself a perfect period piece, with large comfortable rooms, high ceilings, and in our case, I remember an enormous, fully nine- or ten-feet-long, bathtub. The ambience of Rome defies description in a few words, but we certainly enjoyed it as we made plans for site seeing and places to eat. The planning was lackadaisical and we felt no need to rush about. In the two days spent in the Eternal City, I am not sure what sightseeing we accomplished or what dining adventures we had, but we certainly had our own dreamy *Roman Holiday.*[14]

CHAPTER THIRTEEN

ARABIAN DAYS

My total association with *Arabian Nights* before visiting the Middle East was a half-forgotten brush with childish cartoons. I had seen characterizations such as: *Ali Baba and Forty Thieves* or *Simbad the Sailor*. However, I was prepared to observe a profound cultural shift in my "Arabian days."

Of course, the very name "Middle East" lumping together, as it does, cities such as Cairo and Teheran that are distant on so many measures, proclaims a Eurocentric view. The Middle East (sometimes called Near East) and Far East exist as categories created in Europe. But there is no doubt that the characterizations *Europe* and *Middle East* have descriptive value of the distinctive political and cultural differences. The thirst to understand the world, the dreams of travel and the ambitions created in my youthful mind by reading about those distant places, was about to be fulfilled. In addition, every radio station and every popular artist seemed, at that time, to be performing *Those Far Away Places*—a hymn to my dreams.[15]

The practical concerns were, not so much about political powers or of police states we might encounter, but whether those who would interface with our aircraft operations were to be dependable in the same way as at home base. I knew that some of the BOAC station engineers would be my friends from the Irish Army Air Corps, and others would be like the stolid characters I knew at Heathrow in London. But the list of those we had to interface with included station engineers, baggage handlers, refuel mechanics, air traffic controllers, and so on—all of whom in the context of aviation must perform at a high level. For example, it might seem at first sight, that baggage handlers could be compared to laborers in other industries, where just physical labor is required. But with aircraft, they bear responsibility for properly handling cargo doors. A loss of a cargo door in flight would lead to an explosive decompression and possible loss of the aircraft.

There was an unspoken but widespread concern that the Middle East and beyond might supply a more mercurial support staff than the personalities we were used to. We viewed Middle Eastern and Far Eastern cultures to be more imbued with authoritarianism and fatalism, and we wondered if this would impact our operations.

An incident I recall illustrates why we had a high level of interest in the performance of the people who would support us. On approach to a waypoint, in this case, the intersection of two VOR vectors, I idly listened to our ATC clearance. A little later, the radio traffic from ATC gave clearance to another aircraft that sounded similar—so I hit the intercom switch and asked, "Captain did ATC just clear the other aircraft to the same time and altitude at the checkpoint?" Sure enough they had!

A disaster in 1970 with an aircraft I had flown first on the 10 June 1959 and many times afterward, further highlights the reliance the flight crew must place on support roles, and the danger of adhering to routines when there is uncertainty about the underlying conditions. Dan Air Flight 1903 flying the Comet 4, G-APDN, departed Manchester at 16:08 hours on 3 July 1970 for Barcelona. When overflying the Paris area, the pilot had to alter the routing in his flight plan. After contact with Barcelona at 17:53 it was agreed that the aircraft would fly past the Sabadell beacon, about fourteen miles north of the airfield, and turn left descending to intersect the centerline of the runway, about twelve miles east of the airfield, at 6,000 feet altitude.

From the point of view of communications, the remarkable element that can be elicited from the radio transmissions transcript, is that both the pilot and the air traffic controller were uncertain about the pilot's estimates of the time for passing the Sabadell beacon, *but when he mistakenly declared he had passed it, they both accepted that he had.* A fateful and irrevocable decision was made in an instant. The captain turned left, the aircraft made a CFIT (controlled flight into terrain) some forty miles north of where it should have been. All 112 lives aboard were lost; the passengers with no warning, but the pilot probably came to the realization of doom after the die was cast, and no amount of engine power or maneuvering would save the day. A fascinating aspect of this tragedy was the lack of use of DME. Knowing accurately the distance to the airport would be very powerful in pointing out a thirty mile navigational error.

Bahrain is an island in the Persian Gulf. Its ancient traditions owe a debt to Ali Baba, and at present it lies in the heart of Arab and Islamic influence. I looked forward with great interest to stopovers there, and to broadening my experience of how other lives were lived.

The island kingdom was then a British protectorate. That is, its external affairs were the responsibility of Britain, while the internal administration was local and strictly Islamic. Now of course, such a division of powers can never be seamless, and the first intimation we had of some realpolitik compromise was on the importation of liquor. The state religion strictly forbade any alcohol, but the many resident and visiting Westerners wished to enjoy a drink. The solution in our case, we understood to be, that stewardesses could *get by* customs with a partial bottle of liquor and men should have none. While this seemed to produce the desired behavior, it appeared to be utterly ridiculous to us Westerners.

Alcoholism is a pervasive problem. In my family my mother, a widow, fretted that her *mere* feminine authority would be insufficient to protect her boys from waywardness, particularly with "drink." She was, however, clear that authoritarianism was dysfunctional. Everyone knew of the failed American top down, authoritarian experiment with prohibition of liquor in the 1920s, and the increase in crime it created. Infused with my homely values, virtue would be having lots of liquor and the interior disposition to use it wisely.

There can be no disagreement that civic authority must protect the weak from the strong and punish the criminals; but again, the local administration of Bahrain was entirely at odds with our way of thinking on punishment. For example, the penalty for theft was the amputation of the thief's right hand. We understood, that like the liquor question, there was a realpolitik solution. The RAF kept an aircraft at the ready to fly out Westerns accused of petty crime, since the imposition of such barbaric punishments would be disruptive in a way unwanted by British *and local* authorities.

The airport in Bahrain was located on the island, Muharraq, north of the main island and capitol city. The airport itself was a combination of an international airport and a RAF base. On stopovers we were accommodated adjacent to the airport, and this remote location turned out to be very interesting. Our stays in Bahrain were pleasant, untouched by trepidation about the local administration or anti-British Arab Nationalism social unrest that was under way in the city at that time. Comfortable as we were with royalty as a figurehead in England, we were uncertain how to view a strongman like Al-Khalifa and his British advisor who governed the Island. Indeed, schooled in the French Revolutionary ideals, it was difficult to ascribe them *any* legitimacy. The authoritarian climate contrasted with our liberal views of economics, education, and certainly with government's role in the enforcement of ethics and morals.

In the evenings, the crews got together for the customary social gathering. These gatherings were truly about socializing, not about drinking. But the illicit liquors played a useful part. In the daytime, I undertook to walk for exercise and to get the *feel* of the neighborhood. Muharraq island was a desert setting. Walking in the well populated neighborhood one was immediately made aware of a stillness, an eerie unrelieved *lack* of bustle. The houses were walled off by high blank walls and only a fleeting glimpse of their human dimensions could be seen through the iron gates that guarded the entrances. Strolling past these walled compounds gave one the uneasy feeling that only inside could human sanctuary be found. The experience served to immerse me in the *otherness* of this culture. It was similar to when I was a little kid and walked warily around fairy forts. We had no belief in fairies as such, but our minds were excited by the terror of the unknown.

This brief brush with a different society and culture alerted me to the fragility of the principles we took for granted. and to ponder what life would be like without them. I had a strong feeling that our cherished principles of separation of spiritual and civic powers, democracy, and freedom were inverted and life there must involve either silent acquiescence or a Hobbesian struggle of individual against everyone else. It was a disquieting thought experiment.

CHAPTER FOURTEEN

THE PARIS OF THE MIDDLE EAST

Our Comet 4 fleet serviced many places of the Middle East. Some of these, such as Aden, Damascus, Abadan, and Kuwait, were stops for passengers and refueling only. Of the cities where we had stopovers, I think that most of us would pick Beirut as their favorite. Beirut, due to culture, climate, history, location, and other indefinable elements, presented a highly attractive ambience for visitors. In recent history, it had been under a German and then a French mandate. It was home to a vibrant Lebanese Christianity and a Muslim majority. It had become a financial capitol and playground for wealthy Arab princes. The delightful lively city was undoubtedly a severe contrast to the working environment of many youthful sheiks. The French mandate had ended in 1943; but with one foot in Europe and one foot in the Middle East, many liked to call it, "the Paris of the Middle East."

For us the Bristol Hotel was home-away-from-home. In accord with the English class system pilots were housed at the nearby Carleton Hotel. This pluralistic prosperous city was the home of a lively café scene, but BOAC had, in essence, its own watering hole a short distance from these hotels. The Golden Bar fulfilled the role of the "local" in British parlance. Beirut was a stopover on routes to the Middle East, Far East, and Australia, guaranteeing that there were always two or three Comet 4 crews in town, and a diverse set of friends or acquaintances at the Golden Bar.

In the evenings, if one was not in the eight-hour pre-flight alcohol abstention period, it was common to wend one's way to the Golden Bar. In this cosmopolitan city, the bar was stocked with anything you might ask for, but by a huge margin the most popular drink was gin and tonic. It owed some of its popularity to the belief that tonic was either a good or an essential guard against malaria.

The barroom conversation was heavily skewed to aviation topics. With the crews thrown together for short periods of intensive activity, people tended to live an airline life separated from a home life. In the Golden Bar, I heard of a captain who succeeded in having a particular stewardess assigned to all his trips. They, of course, slept together. He was supposedly, otherwise successfully married to a "home" wife, so it appeared that he was the high-tech personification of *The Captain's Paradise*— but without the comedy.[16] This lack of comedy did not prevent a lot of humorous speculation. It might seem that with a group of women selected for their attractiveness that stories of this kind abounded, however, it was not the case. While there was undoubtedly sexual misconduct, there was little promiscuity or romance among the group. My friend Terry Hardeman married a stewardess from another airline, but their courtship was in London in their time off.

Another story that was followed with intense interest in the Golden Bar, concerned the "mutiny" of a Comet 4 crew. As the rumor mill told it, the first officer and crew observed the captain's excessive use of alcohol, in other words, it affected his flying. Then on final approach to Calcutta's Dum Dum airport, *he appeared* to *be lining up the aircraft on street lights rather than the runway lights.* The first officer saw to a safe landing, but the whole crew agreed they would fly no further with that captain. They were all flown back to London where an inquiry was held.

A day time recreational area was available at the Saint George Marina. One could order drinks and snacks, read or sit and converse. In those days, the recreational area of the club and Marina was an elevated pier, with sun umbrellas and lounge chairs where we wore bathing suits and enjoyed the sunshine. I first went there expecting the "Mediterranean beach" of my imagination—wide expanses of sand and gentle waves. But I found instead of a beach, a vertical pier wall with lashing waves. The water level varied almost ten feet between ebb and flow. An anchored steel ladder descended the face of the wall, and I thought I could safely use that to at least get my bathing suit wet. Adventurously, I went down a few steps and was pummeled, I then thought I will swim, rising and falling, next to the ladder. But the moment I released my grip on the ladder I knew I had made a bad mistake; as the next wave rose it washed back from the wall separating me from the ladder by about ten feet.

On my third try to regain the ladder, I was close to despair. I might not succeed in that turmoil of swirling waters! In this spirit of anxiety, I made a desperate, unstinting effort and found the ladder. I maintained a deathly grip on it, as the waters sloshed up and down and my left foot was gashed by the rough wall. I gratefully ascended firmly rung by rung, with the water washed over my head. I climbed out and joined the others sipping their cocktails, and lounging under the brightly colored umbrellas. But I was disjointed from their conversation; from my brush with near drowning my mind was attuned to "life is not going to last forever." I had, in a few minutes, lost some of that unthinking youthful attitude that we are invincible.

Besides the social evenings in the Golden Bar or sunbathing at the Saint-George Marina, Beirut had many other attractions. The city was safe and could be explored on foot. Taxis were cheap and plentiful. Coming from a society where blowing your horn was reserved for emergencies, it was noticeable that the streets continuously echoed beep-beep, beep-beep. My imagination suggested the drivers were just a happy bunch, a judgment in consonance with their genial interactions in general.

The American University Beirut (AUB) is a powerful institution situated in the city, and within easy walking distance of the Bristol hotel. Having married an American girl, but with little exposure to American culture I was naturally very curious. A unique aspect of the culture became apparent to me when I stopped to watch at a playing field populated by an excited group of men and boys. It was indeed very edifying to see the father/son baseball game proceed with such great delight all around. I deemed it to be a uniquely American tradition.

A visit to the Bazaar was endlessly interesting, even if, as in my case, I was too frugal to go on a shopping binge. We organized memorable tours to Damascus, Baalbek, and Byblos. These were easily arranged by taxi. At the Syrian border, there were heavily armed check points, and a militaristic climate that was a stark contrast to peaceful Lebanon. Naively, many of us were convinced that the Lebanese had a unique working political arrangement for Christian-Muslim coexistence that bypassed a demand for a unitary Islamic state. With the hindsight of history, we know that beginning in 1975 their peaceful prosperous society would begin to unravel.

CHAPTER FIFTEEN

A SHIA CAPITOL

Through the many ancient imperial dynasties that ruled in Persia, Iran, of course, has a very different cultural heritage from the Arabian countries. I came face to face with the distant past of Persian culture in conversations with a vivacious Iranian stewardess. She felt some fellowship with me, thinking of us as being similarly religious minorities. Her father functioned in the keeping of a Zoroastrian perpetual flame that had existed from antiquity. We had a number of interesting religious and philosophical discussions. Ever afterwards, I wondered about the theological implications of the flame being extinguished.

The questions about cultural differences were highlighted in a different way on my first arrival in Teheran. On 1 February 1960 we left London before midnight, transited Rome, and I arrived for my first time in Teheran mid-morning. We cleared customs and immigration and our crew of eight, four flight deck crew, the English cabin staff, and two Iranian stewardesses, boarded the crew bus for a trip to our downtown hotel. At that time, the main highway from Mehrabad Airport to downtown Tehran was a four-lane road with an elevated grassy median strip. The median strip was crowded with merchants selling watermelons and other produce. I surveyed the scene with great interest, the lively open air market and the turbaned merchants, raised my expectations of a new experience.

But I was soon to be jolted from my complacency. After leaving the airport we encountered stop-and-go traffic while the opposing traffic from the city to the airport was very light. After a few minutes of braking and edging forward our driver bumped the bus over the curb and across the grassy strip between the merchants, and drove the *wrong way* down the other carriageway. When oncoming traffic appeared, I was unsure if he would continue and force it off the road or just into the slow lane, but no, in a calculated move he jumped the curb again and found his way back between the merchants to the correct side. It seemed with head-on closing speeds of possibly eighty to one hundred miles per hour the young man driver was playing with destiny for no good reason. Then he repeated the crazy maneuver all over again. I pondered to myself, was it bravado? Bad judgment? However, I concluded because of the acceptance of his behavior—there were no yelling and screaming merchants and there was stoicism on the part of the crew—there was a cultural aspect, a way of life, to his behavior. What, I asked myself, if the driver's brother was our refuel mechanic, or his cousin was our flagman directing our aircraft on the tarmac?

On arrival at the hotel, the manager collected our passports—that night these would be inspected by the state police. Accompanying each passport must be a note stating the bearers religion. An awkward moment ensued as the manager asked that each one state their religion. The first says "Church of England," I say, "Roman Catholic," a third says, "No religion." This third crew member like all of us was an infidel in Muslim terms, but I surmised that he would not have positive religious views that should give offence to anyone; he surely was not a steadfast atheist or a flaming communist with religious views about destiny and eschatology. I guessed that growing up he was encouraged merely not to be *naughty*. It could have been he was truly a man whose interior life was lacking a concept of the supernatural. But the manager's facial expression made it clear that such things could not be committed to paper. In the pause that followed, our crewman muttered, "C of E (Church of England)." The remainder of the crew, one by one, happily agreed: "C of E."

This first arrival in Tehran was on an eastbound leg. On many visits to that city I arrived there on a westbound flight from New Delhi. These latter sectors I learned to respect as they illustrated the complexity of the many practical considerations about the personal use of time. What follows here is a fictitious account of such a westbound leg, based upon the experiences of actual trips.

It is Sunday 8:45 p.m. in New Delhi, and I shut down the engines—high pressure fuel cocks first, then the low pressure fuel cocks. Then follows a number of measures to secure the aircraft. I close the log by entering the arrival time: 15:15 GMT. It had been an uneventful flight so there was no need for a conference with the station engineer or notes to be left for the next flight engineer taking over.

We had flown from Hong Kong by way of Bangkok and had been on duty for about ten hours. Taking my seat on the bus, I share with the others a sense of satisfaction. Our feeling was that we had met our goal: the shepherding of a incredibly complex piece of equipment through an exceedingly intricate journey with such élan that our clients had hardly noticed.

An hour later, our crew were checking into the *fabulous* Ashoka Hotel, set as it is in the Indian capitol's diplomatic area as a showcase for Indian hospitality. At the desk, I check the crew mail and I am the delighted recipient of an "aerogram" from home.

Captain Wells, briefcase in hand, and about to get in the elevator says, "See you guys for dinner." So after a quick change and wash-up we join him in the dining room. With the six of us around the table the conversation has an end-of-day lethargy, so we generally settle for listening to the musical ensemble that played during the dinner time. At first come classical pieces, and then it morphs to Indian melodies. The Indian entertainment includes a young woman dancer who incredibly performs a wildly energetic dance on a brass plate. As the pleasing well-known classical strains fade, Janet, our stewardess, wrinkles her nose. "Aha" she says, "Indian!" But the Indian melodies are nostalgic to my ears, they are same melodies my uncles played when I was child as Indian and Irish music enjoy a common lineage from the Celts.

Monday I was not in a hurry and just managed to get breakfast before the kitchen closed. After breakfast there was an opportunity to enjoy the swimming pool, but I was thinking ahead that we must prepare for our midnight departure to Tehran! So, by early afternoon I darkened the room and retired to bed. This *effort* to rest is not as hopeless as it might seem. I had gotten used to odd schedules and time zone changes. Still, I was already up when the hotel desk called about 9 o'clock. The crew are packed, uniformed, checked out, and waiting in the lobby for the crew transport shortly after 10 o'clock. Just before midnight I was chatting with the ground crew and making pre-flight inspections.

On the flight deck everything is normal. The GPU (Ground Power Unit) and our inverters are producing low and high voltage to power our radios and instrumentation. I start the fuel log. Fuel readings are showing the that fuel and weight (AUW) for the flight plan agreed with the captain's preflight briefing. We are ready for departure! With doors closed the first officer checks with the control tower for permission to start our engines.

As we complete the familiar checklists everything is in place. It requires an act of will to *not just* repeat the verifying phrase but to truly verify by observing or touching the controls. Each engine starts with a familiar satisfying whine. Given the cool morning ambience the JPT's (jet pipe temperatures) stay well below the 800 degree limit, and the appropriate needles swing into position in their gauges. The first officer calls for the taxi instructions while I check all system indicators, both on the engineer's panel and the pilot's panels, all needles sit steady in their proper range. The captain calls "chocks away," on Tuesday 00:47 o'clock the flight is underway.

As we swing onto the active runway, the captain and first officer both place their hands on the fully open throttles. I check engine RPMs, fuel flows, and JPTs, and call out "full power four engines." In moments, while we accelerate, the first officer calls V1 and shortly thereafter V2. We reduce engine power as we climb out at 260 knots IAS (nautical miles per hour, indicated airspeed). I introduce cabin pressurization. Since the airfield has an elevation of less than 1000 feet, I allow the cabin pressure altitude to climb slowly toward my target of 6000 feet.

The Comet 4 is equipped with engines capable of 42000 pounds of thrust at sea level, which could, if the Captain chose, climb like a fighter plane. However, our ascent is more leisurely, as we follow ATC permitted flight levels that would maintain 1000-foot vertical separation with opposing traffic.

By about 01:30 a.m. we reach our cruise altitude of 36,000 feet. Again we run through our checklist as we begin the cruise portion of the flight. I scan my own and the pilots systems—hydraulics, electrics, fuel, warning systems, pressurization, cabin air, basic flying instruments. The radio reports no weather of consequence en route, so I expect the next three hours should be routine, checking the waypoints, logging fuel and weight, and being alert to any indications of malfunction.

I peer out the windscreen. With no moon, the vault of the sky is pitch black, and the largely uninhabited terrain below our flight path gives no evidence of human habitation. We know that the inky blackness outside, only inches from our heads, is a very hostile place. A human body would be shattered instantly in the extremely cold low-pressure atmosphere. But the flight deck is a cozy familiar spot, no more threatening than a comfortable piece of ye olde England on a summer afternoon, say Richmond Park with a view of the Thames burbling past.

Ah! It is clear these thoughts are trouble! The demon sleep is attacking me. As I push the reverie aside, it is immediately clear that my brain and "I" are not working as one. I put on my oxygen mask—some O_2 will help! Now, self preservation suggests I check the two figures in the left and right seats; they seem O.K. but I note the first officer also has his oxygen mask on.

The sleep demon pushes me harder, so I decide to splash cold water upon my face! I press the intercom switch:

"Captain I'm going to the bathroom."

"Your panel O,K.?"

"Yessir, it's all set, I need to dash some water on my face."

"Good idea."

I did not like admitting any weakness on my part, but good crew communications require that facts be stated. I make a determined effort to again finesse fuel temperatures and check that booster pump selections are good for the time being before I move my creaky limbs to stand up. I push past the flight deck curtain and into the bathroom. Ah! The liberal use of cold water on the face and neck seems to be working, so I return to the flight engineer's station.

But as I sit down I find my eyelids closed, so I exert willpower to open them. Only sheer effort keeps my head upright. As my mind struggles I am flooded with people and scenes from what I take to be mind "rhythms" somewhere between my willed consciousness and my autonomous functioning. Is that my mother scolding her little boy, in a meadow scene at Richmond Park? My head droops involuntarily, and my neck muscles crack a they halt my head's downward slump. This shock allows me to refocus. So, starting at the top of the panel I look to the Green hydraulic system reservoir indicator for one whole second that seems like an eternity, before my deadened senses can conclude that it is O.K. Blue hydraulic system? No response from my deadened mind! As a mixed sense of despair and terror claws at my mind I decide this scan is not really functioning. I debate continuing the scan, maybe, hopefully, *yes, hopefully* I would find something wrong and get a needed injection of adrenalin? The more my mind insists on bodily performance, the more the sides of my head hurt. My eye-lids and neck muscles only obey sporadically, so I conclude, my best bet is to stand up! I slip the belt buckle and lean far forward to ease the effort to become upright. With willpower I am standing. The scene through the windscreen shows the zenith still inky black, but I distinguish a line on the horizon like a crack in a china plate. I realize that it is the mountain peaks backlit by first light, jagged onyx mountains with a faint solar radiance pushing into the arc of the black sky. Instantaneously, well, within five seconds, there is what seems a miraculous event: my diurnal cycle kicks in. I am not just observing a solar radiance: a life force is flowing back into my limbs and mind, and the "I" is in charge again. There will be no trouble meeting our performance goals.

Arriving in Tehran was always pleasant. The city was architecturally pleasing and laid out with wide boulevards and beautiful lush vegetation. To the north the a spectacular vista of snowy Alborz mountain peaks creates an extraordinary ambience for the living experience.

But when I think of Tehran I am also reminded of the story told to me by my friend John. John was a first officer and we had met on several trips and participated in sightseeing activities together. Over a cup of coffee in Tehran he recounted his previous trip to Tokyo: these Tokyo trips kept a crew together for up to three weeks. Whenever the crew got together, John explained, the captain dominated the conversation. No matter what the topic was, the captain always had definitive opinions, proclaimed them strongly, and had the last word. John said, "I could have tolerated it but for the fact that he was always right!" When they arrived in Tehran, the last night before their return to London, the crew ate at a dinner/dance club. After they were seated the captain offered a criticism of the violin player in the orchestra. The crew in exasperation unanimously agreed, "Well why don't *you* do it correctly." The final straw was, the captain acquiesced. He headed off to consult the orchestra leader and the astounded crew next saw him on stage, where in John's unprofessional opinion, he fiddled away satisfactorily.

CHAPTER SIXTEEN

A CITY ON THE NILE

Many years earlier, I had learned about Egyptian antiquities and mythology. Who could not be amazed and intrigued? A young mind awakening to the nature of the world has to be open minded, and I was fascinated with the Egyptian ideas about the continuity of this life with the next life. The ancient Egyptians thought they had pierced the veil of death—an exploration of the unseen spirit world that was a necessary accompaniment of the physical environment. Egyptian mythology clearly raises the perpetual question—what is the meaning of human existence? So, the antiquities of Egypt were intriguing, and I was very excited at the prospect of visiting Cairo.

It was not possible, given the length of our stopovers, to arrange for trips to Luxor or Alexandria, but Cairo has many places of interest. Of major interest, is the Sphinx and pyramids at Giza. At that time, the tourist trade was not heavy and a small bus ran from downtown Cairo to a dusty desert stop a short distance from the pyramids. At the pyramid, a man collected, it seemed apologetically, a small fee; and un-shepherded tourists like me were free to wander. My attention was attracted to a cordoned-off area where there was an archeological dig, and then to an unused passageway. I entered hesitantly, it was narrow, rocky, and dark; and I wondered had I stumbled into a place I was not supposed to be. I gave very careful thought to the question: could I easily retrace my steps outward at any time? In the spirit of flight engineering preparedness, I had with me a small pocket flashlight. This lit my way. Like a bolt of lightning it struck me! I was headed to a burial chamber at the center of the pyramid. After ascent up a debris-strewn narrow passage that seemed to be crumbling in places, I arrived there and found it lit by a reddish bare 25-watt lamp dangling from a cord—hardly enough light to dispel a fraction of the complete blackness. I could barely distinguish the slab that formed the top of the 4500-year-old sarcophagus. Given the lighting, I saw no more of the walls as would an occupant of the coffin.

As any tourist, I had my camera with color film, probably the film speed was 25 ASA. The lighting was inadequate! As an experiment, I placed the camera on the sarcophagus opened the shutter and stood for a minute or two before closing the shutter. In this way, I actually did get an image of myself.

After World War Two, there was a general withdrawal by European Powers from administration in the Middle East leading to many unstable political developments, and violent outcomes. The Suez Canal since its completion in 1869, like the Panama Canal had super-national importance. In that time, before supertankers were hauling huge quantities oil round the west coast of Africa, England and France foresaw their economies could be hugely impacted by restrictions of the Suez route. There was also rivalry between Egypt and Iraq for the hegemony of the Arab world. Israel suffered continual murderous raids on civilians, and their commercial shipping was blockaded from the Suez Canal and the Straits of Tiran. In October 1956, Israel, France, and Britain attacked Egypt, but a ceasefire was declared by November, and British forces were withdrawn on December 22nd to be replaced by UNEF troops, a United Nations Emergency Force, a force established by the General Assembly to secure an end to the Suez Crisis. This was the political prelude to my arrival on BOAC Flight 932 on 8 August 1960, after commercial relations had been reestablished.

I expected a routine process through immigration and customs, but on this occasion to my utter surprise, I was in Cairo and my passport was in London. There was good reason to be apprehensive about the Egyptian response to a lack of proper paperwork. I debated would they treat it as minor matter, or insist on incarceration until the passport arrived? I sought out our station manager who cabled London and did not seem to favor my getting back on the plane. I am not sure what really happened, but in the immigration processing, the crew had to pass along a counter handing in their passports and then their Inoculation records at different stations, and then picking them up at different stations further along. I passed through this process without passport or incident—I suspect entirely by coincidence.

Safely past immigration and customs, I boarded the crew transport for the hotel; then known as the Nile Hilton. The hotel had been opened in 1958 as a touch of Americana in the new postwar Egypt. The luxurious space and unparalleled service was not just about America but projected an aura of hopeful possibilities in a world that just made history by shedding the continuous state of war. It was in fact, another uplifting aspect of the spirit that created the Comet 4.

Next morning, I opted for breakfast in my room, consoling myself that this would be better than any food served in detention! And indeed, it was; it arrived on a trolley that became a table with fine linen and silver, while the food was served hot from a warming oven. My mother would be hard pressed to produce a better bacon and eggs. Sometime after breakfast there was a knock on the door; it was the delivery of a package with my passport. BOAC had jumped hastily into action. A surprised Catherine, had the previous evening fetched the passport from the pocket of my spare uniform for their courier.

Cairo was a cosmopolitan city. The people were friendly and there were lots of interesting things to do. Beyond the Sphinx and Pyramids at Giza there were museums full of antiquities. There were also pleasant places to meet with friends for coffee or a meal.

On a trip in July 1960, I arrived in Cairo and had a leisurely evening. Next day I was due to fly flight 755 to London. Naturally, my mind turned to thoughts of my beloved in Twickenham, and to the anticipation of her meeting my airplane. I knew I was a better technician than poet but, of course, these categories are not reductive! And I saw no barrier to attempting to express the ineffable. Taking a sheet of Nile Hilton stationery, I tried to set down my thoughts:

> *I love you Kit*
> *A simple statement.*
> *Too simple.*
> *I can use poetic language*
> *Though I am not a poet—*
> *Not in a proper sense.*

If I use poetic language,
Then maybe I am a poet?—
Without ability.
Without discipline!

As I begin to lose the train of thought
That caused me first to write.
But that is because
Each little thing about US
Seems important enough to discuss.
To explain important

I wish you well
happiness, laughter
holiness, perfection, justice
well being, fulfillment
fun, children, and a good husband
I want to know you
And you to know me
In the present
In the past
In the future
What is above
may not look like logic
But I feel it is there if only you could see it
Tomorrow I see you
That's logic[17]

CHAPTER SEVENTEEN

AFRICAN JOURNEYS

I was familiar with the phrase "the darkest Africa;" as it implied an ultimate of some kind. Obviously, one interpretation related the phrase to the terrifying tropical jungles, so overgrown that daylight could not penetrate. But in my mind, it stood as well for my ignorance of things African. Beyond Egypt, to the south lay the great civilization, Ethiopia, and to the west the tribal life of the great desert: an immense continent beyond was in the process of freeing itself from colonial governance but also enmeshed in fruitless little understood genocidal wars.

Arriving in a Comet 4 jetliner to dispel ignorance would surely be very unlike Henry Morton Stanley's enlightenment in his journey to find the heroic Dr. Livingstone, when in 1871, the New York Herald commissioned him to search for the missing British hero. There would be no opportunity to trudge the interior of the "Dark Continent" on

121

foot over the "myriad" of "ridges" and say, "Dr. Livingstone, I presume." My view of Africa would be confined almost entirely to spanking-new airports and hotels.

BOAC operated Comet 4 services to Tripoli, Benghazi, Khartoum, Nairobi, Salisbury, Johannesburg, Dakar, Kano, and Lagos. However, crew stopovers were only at Johannesburg and Khartoum on flights to South Africa. Stopovers on flights to Nigeria were at Lagos, while stopovers were at Dakar before crossing the South Atlantic Ocean to Recife for destinations in South America.

Our main service to South Africa presented an interesting example of the vagaries of crew scheduling. Leaving London, we flew three sectors to a stopover in Khartoum. On leaving Khartoum we flew three sectors to a stopover in Johannesburg. The sectors averaged about two and one half hours each. The trip home was similarly six sectors, followed by two days off. Flight crews did not do this consecutively, but cabin crews who repeated this schedule continuously found it too draining, and had to be given a more mixed duty roster.

Johannesburg is appropriately titled ,"The City of Gold" since it was founded as part of the Witwatersrand gold rush of 1886, and continued to be the largest center of gold production. I recall my first arrival in Johannesburg. As usual, I was curious to get the feel of the city. English was in use everywhere, so there were no concerns about language. I explored the downtown area by walking and taking the bus in an aimless fashion. Arriving at the end of a bus line, I determined to catch a bus returning in the direction I had come, fearing I might end up, by mishap, in a dangerous ghetto. And then something amazing happened. I spotted an apartheid sign, which said, "Whites only on this side," and I had a completely unexpected visceral angry impulse to tear it down. Of course, good sense prevailed. I knew of apartheid before arriving in South Africa, and it had seemed that it should not be of concern to me—until that sign touched some deeply felt emotions about the nature and dignity of human life.

My reaction to the apartheid sign was a lesson on race relations. But a deeper view of race relations was to be afforded me on a gold mine tour. These mines were then the deepest in the world, so a small group of us with some curiosity signed up for a gold mine tour. We expected to be impressed by the unique winding machinery and the underground equipment for boring and roof bolting. We who had been 40,000 feet in the air would like to add to our résumé 10,000 feet under the earth.

We were certainly impressed by the colossal winding engine and noted that the cage speed was 1,800 feet per minute. On the Comet 4, the cabin pressure altitude was manually controlled by the flight engineer and we strove to never exceed 500 feet per minute rate of climb or descent. 1800 feet per minute would be ear popping!

Our tour was unique in the sense that our guide did not speak from a prepared text. The tour guide was a middle manager, who seemed more interested in a two-way conversation with our aviation group than an exposition of each feature we visited. We descended to the lowest level and were disappointed to discover that the trek to the working face would be too far. The First Aid room and equipment at the lowest level elicited interest. It raised questions about the injury statistics for the mine; the comparable rates for the in mine injuries and fatalities for miners to the rates in their homeland setting, and the hazardousness of mining in general. We could see parallels between mining and aviation: an elevated potential for disasters with searing headlines and multiple deaths. As a graduate of BOAC survival training for the possibilities of a forced landing or ditching at sea, I grappled with possible types of underground contingences. Apart from disasters, our group had interest in occupational hazards, such as whether deep mining has an environmental problem similar to the increased gamma ray exposure of high flying.

The mine used migrant labor from a remote territory, with a new cohort of young men being initiated and trained every six months. To be acceptable, recruits had to pass a medical evaluation and a type of IQ test. The latter consisted, in part, of the ability to place different shaped pegs in an appropriately matching hole.

The main part of the tour was devoted to the lives of the migrant miners. What was surprising was the paternalism of the arrangements given our predilection to see coercion and exploitation. The miners after their six-month participation in the cash economy were returned to their homeland. While on the job, their accommodations, food, health care, and recreation were taken care of in a somewhat militaristic fashion. Our guide pointed out with pride the quality of the food and accommodations. He offered a sample of the "home" brewed beer. Our tour ended visiting with a couple I will call Grandma and Grandpa. On the property, was a well-furnished bungalow where lived the older couple. This was the home of two permanent employees from the miner's homeland whose job was to provide a sympathetic ear if needed to the young men.

The city of Khartoum, that was our stopover on trips to and from Johannesburg, is situated at the confluence of the White Nile and the Blue Nile. This in itself, should make a visit there attractive. The idea of the Nile River as mother of a civilization nurturing hunter-gatherers to an agricultural, famine banishing society comes readily to mind.

Such romanticism was banished on arrival in Khartoum airport. There was no hint of the cruel civil war that was raged in the Sudan, but a coercive atmosphere pervaded the place. I think it began with immigration procedures, there instead of viewing and stamping our passports they just confiscated them on entry, to be returned only when departing. We were housed in a BOAC house with meals in a dining room and a bar for convivial evenings. I know of no crew member who ventured beyond the compound except to board the crew transport to the airport.

In those days, Lagos was the capitol city of Nigeria. At Lagos, I cannot remember any sightseeing activities; the short stay and hot climate discouraged any adventurous impulses. The city is associated in my mind with a particular preflight inspection, as the aircraft sat on the tarmac in the noonday sun in the month of April. In my inspection I noted that, for the only time in my flying experience, that the outside air temperature (OAT) was out of limits.

I sought out the captain and said, "Look this OAT is outside the engine operating range." At 43 degrees, Celsius it had exceeded the upper limit of the textbook ambient air temperature for our Avon engines. Captain Jenkins nodded wordlessly; I guess the oppressive heat and humidity was making it difficult to vocalize the possibly balmier conditions on the open runway! There was no noticeable difference in the start-up and running of the engines. We took off without incident, but I exercised a little more caution when I proclaimed, "full power four engines."

Plate tectonics tells us that over 100,000,000 years ago Lagos, Nigeria; and Recife, Brazil were in the same neighborhood, but now Dakar was the airline gateway to cross the Atlantic to South America. The flight time of the Comet 4 to cross the South Atlantic to Recife or Natal was about four hours and thirty minutes. A non-stop from Dakar to Rio de Janeiro took about seven hours.

Dakar was a city of contrasts. I found a dazzling contrast in the merchandizing of French pastries and meat. The French pastry shop that enticed me inside was fronted by a hot dusty street. Entering the glass door, one entered into a store that might have been on a Parisian boulevard; pristine clean and cool. I noted the remarkable absence of even an occasional house fly. The combination glass counter/display cabinet offered a delightful selection of pastries and cakes. Nearby on that dusty street I was confronted with a boy selling meat. The seven- to ten-year old child was running around waving a piece of meat in his bare hands. The meat looked like a two-pound cut of chateaubriand; *covered in blowflies*. It made one think twice before ordering steak for dinner at our hotel.

The downtown area also contrasted with the native village where native artisans lived and produced goods for sale. Downtown was a collection of buildings of a type that reminded me of a country town in Ireland. The village, a short bus ride away, was populated with native huts that served as living space, artisan studio, and shopping display. The shop keepers were very friendly and engaged readily in conversation; so that the atmosphere was not one of pressure selling but of having an enjoyable discussion with an artist. Although the general merchandise was not of interest to me, I did take an interest in a carving of a pair of grazing gazelles. I dickered on the price and purchased them for about eighty percent of the asking price. I had the strong impression there was no scalping the tourist.

CHAPTER EIGHTEEN

FIVE MINUTES

When I first visited Karachi, it was the capitol of Pakistan, though plans were already afoot to shift the capitol to a more stately environment than what was a business, industrial, and colonial setting. A national pride was at work, like that in Brazil where the new Federal District, Brasilia, was being constructed.

In Karachi, BOAC had extensive proprietary crew accommodations. The facility included multiple buildings and grounds complete with tennis courts; providing a complete living environment for eating, sleeping, laundry, and recreation. The rooms there had a unique arrangement, I have never seen replicated. They were arranged in single-story structures with a row of rooms at the front and a matching row at the back. Between the front and back row were bathrooms. Each pair, consisting of a front and back room, shared a bathroom to which access was controlled by an ingenious set of mechanical levers. Simultaneous access was prevented; when one side—front or back—had access the other side was locked out.

For flight crews, Karachi had more the spirit of BOAC than London Airport. Days there were spent in the company of those you were flying with, or in rekindling the acquaintance with those whom you had shared previous experiences.   Like Beirut, Lebanon, it had the aura of an off-duty home. But Karachi was a cocoon. Its downside was that it kept us from exploring Pakistan's largest city. There was a lot to be seen and experienced in Karachi, but it was also, at that time, a place of political and cultural ferment. Pakistan had been an organized country for only thirteen years.   It was thought that, for safety, exploration should be restricted to organized tourist activities.

The facility manager had a swimming pool construction project underway. The method of excavation aroused my curiosity, so I asked about it. He had two squads of workers: shovelers and carriers. The shovelers dug and placed the excavated material on a blanket and then two carriers grasping the corners would carry a loaded blanket to a truck in the driveway. I asked him, why use this difficult and inefficient method? Why not do the obvious, and use wheelbarrows? I expected there had to be a deep-seated cultural or even religious reason. He explained it was just local regulations that he accepted as given in the spirit of making work and reducing unemployment. At first, I thought this was just outmoded thinking from ideas lacking in sound economic principles. On second thoughts, I conceded to him there could be an economic conundrum. Our jetliners, like wheelbarrows, brought economic efficiency but their macroeconomics and social implications remained a mystery.   Furthermore, aircraft innovation, just like wheelbarrows, would provide that less and less crews were needed to fly airplanes.

The tennis courts were popular. Since I had never owned a racquet or played that game, I was content to sit and watch. Despite my tennis naiveté, I was co-opted through the necessity to form a foursome. It was then I discovered that my hand-eye coordination, developed from the hours of handball I played against those local gable walls as a kid, was quite an asset. To my partner's surprise, and just as much to mine, my terrific serves were a winning element in the game.

Karachi will always be associated in my mind with an attempted landing at Karachi International Airport. There I experienced the closest I was to come to the disaster of losing the aircraft; in the argot of accident statistics, a "hull loss." This incident on 13 February 1960 began with our crew taking the transport to the airport in Tokyo, Japan shortly after midnight. Our aircraft, Flight 931, departed Tokyo at 03:05 a.m. and after a five-hour-and forty-five-minute flight arrived in Hong Kong at 07:50 a.m. local time. On arrival, we discovered that there was a problem; the exact nature of which I do not now recall. The problem would require a juggling of aircraft and crews to minimize passenger delay and inconvenience.

Flight Operations consulted with the flight crews, and on the bus ride to the hotel we discussed the options. Any decision would, of course, rest with our captain, Guy Meadows. We knew his decision making was fostered in the crucible of combat, since like many of the BOAC captains, he had been a bomber pilot. This was not something these pilots liked to talk about, but it surely had been a life-changing experience. There was no evidence that any of them suffered PTSD (post-traumatic stress disorder), but I remember one who described flashback reactions to incoming flak when the new landing approach strobe lights were introduced. In a bomber crew's situation, the mission was paramount, and the aircraft's steady course to the target was maintained despite incoming fire. This course of action was not bolstered by an adrenalin rush from a   response, since the aircraft gunners were only there to defend against fighter attacks. A captain's response to the "ack-ack" rounds bursting all around him was to stay the course.

Whatever influence a warrior mentality may have had on the situation in Hong Kong, the upshot was that we were scheduled for Flight 953 leaving later that day. So, we darkened our rooms and got rest as best we could. Flight 953 departed Kai Tac airport at 4:58 PM.

The first sector to Calcutta took five hours and two minutes. We departed Calcutta for Karachi at 8:58 p.m. local time. We had loaded sufficient fuel for the planned flight to Karachi, fuel for one hour of holding (circling) at altitude, and fuel for diversion to Bombay (Mumbai). It was, we anticipated, to be a routine flight.

At about midnight, Pakistan Standard Time, we reached TOD for a straight-in approach to what was known at that time as Karachi International Airport. It was a clear bright moonlit night with no cloud cover. Karachi ATC was broadcasting arrival weather as they cleared us to begin our initial descent. They were reporting good visibility and light winds. At that point, we were number two for landing, behind a Qantas Lockheed Super Constellation. We acquired the ILS signal and set the altimeters to the QFE to accurately show zero height at the runway entry. Now, if the pilot kept the ILS needles crossed—that is a horizontal needle indicating we were following a descent on the three-degree glide slope, and a vertical needle indicating we were maintaining the runway bearing—then we would arrive at the entry of the runway. Before we could complete the landing procedures we would need our "minimums," that is a specified cloud ceiling and a horizontal range of visibility to complete the final maneuvers for landing safely. These minimums were a 300-hundred-foot ceiling and a three-mile visibility.

But there was a problem; Karachi, at that time of the year, was subject to early morning fog. In the steely moonlight we could actually see a blanket of fog not yet at the airport fence.

The radio reported the Qantas flight as down and clear of the runway. Now it was our turn! On final approach, Meadows called for engine power at 4000 RPM, this was a SOP. At this power level, the engines would only take four seconds to spin up to full power if the landing had to be aborted. We entered a thick fog lair, as Meadows flew closely to the ILS, and the first officer scanned the outside scene for any manifestation of the runway. The tense situation was ended by Meadows calling 8,000 RPM, that is full power. He had aborted the landing.

As the aircraft climbed out we discussed the next step. The navigator and first officer were in agreement—"go to Bombay." I confirmed that the fuel needed was available, as well as the holding fuel. Meadows decided we would "go around" and attempt another landing. The navigator demurred, but the captain's decision was firm. There is, of course, no way to know all the factors that influenced his decision. Had he glimpsed the runway lights? We will never know! We now entered a low level flying regime with its huge fuel burn rate. I pointed out, that by the time we landed the Bombay alternate fuel would be used up.

As we did our circuit, we reentered the same tense flying situation as in our first attempted landing, but this time there was more at stake. In addition to the normal flying, such as setting flap extensions and undercarriage lowering, Meadows was paying particularly intense attention to the ILS, and the first officer was scanning the outside as before. I guessed that we were trying to land with zero ceiling and, at most, one-mile visibility. Then the first officer shouted, "I have control," and he advanced the throttles to full power as we aborted our second landing attempt. He declared, "I saw the runway. We were not lined up."

With the shout, "I have control," a shadow of disbelief crossed my mind. But the cold reality was startlingly clear to all the flight deck crew that we had no good options. We faced the imminent dangers of running out of fuel and crash landing. The idea of never experiencing another dawn and potential death by blunt trauma or watery asphyxiation seemed even less horrible than the loss of the aircraft and passengers. I looked at Captain Meadows and was confident that he had the nerve for the all-important requirement to *fly* the craft to its crash landing. The mode of crash landing, and the piloting skills, would be a determinant of the survival rate. His bomber pilot's steely nerves would be very much needed! The final flight maneuvers would have to be made with hydraulically powered flight controls; with running out of fuel and without engine power would there be hydraulic pressure for operating the flight controls? If it came to that, I hoped that the "wind milling" of the engines as Meadows maintained a glide speed greater than the stall speed of ninety knots, would be sufficient to continue the hydraulic pump operation, and avoid the horror of a "dead stick (useless control column)."

On the climb out we discussed our options. We could make another attempt to land at Karachi International. A third attempt seemed the least likely to succeed, as the thick fog had rolled in. We did not have the fuel to climb to and maintain a holding pattern at altitude awaiting the clearing of the fog. Our navigator, thinking as good navigators do, had estimated after the first aborted landing the vectors, time, and fuel to fly to a small military airport about 150 miles from Karachi. We had sufficient fuel for that, but it was not an easy choice. Its short brick-surfaced runway was too short for Comet 4 operations. The airport, Nawabshah, was broadcasting weather close to our minimums, and it was likely to deteriorate. If we attempted to land there, we were leaving the best fire and rescue services behind at Karachi International. Finally, there was no way to tell if we failed to touchdown there, whether we would have fuel for further maneuvers.

We discussed ditching the aircraft in the bay adjacent to the city, where hopefully rescue services would be speedily organized. Ditching was not attractive. Of course, no one had practiced that! Those six-foot swells would be like a series of brick walls to a craft moving at a speed of over one hundred miles an hour, and our stall speed was ninety knots. There was no SOP, no check list for ditching. I thought furiously, how should I configure the aircraft differently than in a normal landing? Before ditching I would switch the fuel dump valves closed in an attempt to keep those flotation devices—the empty wing tanks—from taking on water. Before we alighted the cabin pressurization dump valve would have to be open, otherwise the plug-type doors and escape hatches could be impossible to open, and before we were floating, I would close that pressurization dump valve, which being located in the cargo hold, would become a hole in the bottom of our "boat." There were no good options!

Jill Hodgeson, the stewardess, came on the flight deck and addressed Captain Meadows, "Captain, what can I tell the passengers?" Meadows curtly indicated she should leave and deal with *her* situation. As she passed my station, I sensed her anxiety and thought her situation was worse than ours. She who would be sensitive to the unusual maneuvering of the aircraft was worried about her passengers, but more importantly, the seriousness of the situation would be very apparent to her. Seeing that we were in the middle of a decision process, I grabbed her arm, "just tell them the weather is bad and we have to divert," I said. She nodded with a hint of a smile, even if she was still in the dark she felt part of the crew.

The flight crew had knowledge of a potential disaster and had the duty to work on it. Working under stress the mind often looks for an escape hatch. Refusing to deal with a stressful situation leads to a panicky confusion. Another faulty response is dealing with a genuine, but more solvable problem, or indeed inventing a solvable problem. Luckily in our case, Speedbird 593, were not in the position of United Flight 173 that, as we have described, crashed in Portland, Oregon when it ran out fuel. They had a genuine problem that deflected the crew from dealing with the primary difficulty. Our craft, G-APDE, was functioning normally with no equipment problems to tempt us to lose focus.

A glider instructor once told me a fascinating example of an "inventing a problem" that went like this: he and a pupil set off on a check ride where the pupil's response to an emergency would be evaluated. The glider was launched by a winch. When they were attached to the winch cable and the signal given, the aircraft moved forward and climbed at the correct air speed under the control of the student. At 600 feet altitude, the instructor released the cable to simulate a cable break. The student failed to react and continued in a nose up attitude losing airspeed.

The instructor had hoped for an automatic response, but concerned for the flight attitude correction before stall speed was reached and disaster overtook them he said, "cable break."

The pupil—no response.

The instructor *yells*, "cable break."

Student answers, "I left the refrigerator door open."

The instructor, "I have control."

A sense of duty is not just an ennobling sentiment but an enabling attitude that not only allays panic but introduces a sort of contempt even for death. There was no hint of panic or confusion in our flight crew. A significant aspect of the situation was that a decision must come quickly. Literally, ever second counted. Nawabshah was the best bet!

On final approach to that brick paved runway there, was in scattered cloud. But to our relief we could make out some of the old-fashioned kerosene flares that they were scrambling, on such short notice, to light and demarcate the runway for us. We were at that time using the fuel from the pinion (external pod) tanks, that is the last tanks to be used. I announced our fuel situation as we were on final approach, we would have less than 700 kilos of fuel at touchdown. Meadows had better put it down in one try! He did put it down firmly and called for reverse thrust.

That produced one final challenge. A dense cloud of brick dust blocking the pilots' vision was blown forward by the reverse thrusters. Meadows steered what he thought was straight ahead. As the aircraft slowed down he called, "reverse thrust off" and discovered we were safely at taxi speed *with runway still ahead.* Those retrofitted reverse thrusters were the margin that saved the day. We taxied to the apron and I shut down the engines at 01:20 a.m.

After we had secured the aircraft Meadows pushed his seat back, "Dominic" he said, "when you gave me those fuel numbers you had some for Mum (an English colloquial expression meaning extra in reserve)?"

"Absolutely not!" I cried emphatically, "I would only give the best estimate I could."

Even now that we were safely on the ground he did not like to think it had been *that close*

Luckily, a KLM Fokker Friendship turbo-prop had diverted to Nawabshah after we did, it had sufficient fuel on board for a return flight to Karachi International after the weather cleared. Our passengers disembarked, and Meadows somehow negotiated for their return to Karachi on the smaller KLM aircraft. I believe the KLM captain took them as a courtesy knowing we wanted the absolute minimal possible AUW for takeoff on the short runway, and, besides, Nawabshah was not cleared for Comet 4 operations.

The pilots handled the unloading and loading of the passenger's baggage, and I supervised the refueling for the return to Karachi International. As day broke, the fuel truck arrived—a Toyota truck with four fifty-five-gallon drums, a hand pump, and a hose with a plain nozzle on the end of it. I noted with approval, their carefulness in that they were going to follow "good practice" and strain the fuel through a chamois cloth. The two Pakistani airmen with the truck set to work with good will. Surprisingly, they had no English, but we communicated well.

Normally, refueling was done by oil companies that attach their pumper truck hoses to standardized nozzles concealed under the wings. With the available equipment, we had to use the tank caps on the top of the wings. So, we walked the wing tops to locate the never-used fuel caps. One airman pumped and the other held the dispensing nozzle and the chamois strainer cloth. Whenever the four drums were emptied they would disappear and return shortly. My lack of Urdu and their lack of English did present one problem: The very large, very shallow wing fuel tank looked to the nozzle man to be full and I had difficulty convincing him to continue to pump into it when the fuel level was close to the filler cap.

With the fuel uploaded and the aircraft secured, I climbed inside the empty aircraft. At first, I tried to close my eyes and snooze, but there was nothing farther from my mind than sleep. Jill came to do some work in the galley. I was curious to see her. What, if any, effects our recent adventure had on her thinking? She was a new breed of stewardess. In the beginning when BOAC was Imperial Airways, they hired registered nurses to soothe passengers on their London to Paris service. I supposed that was the thinking behind the adoption of the ubiquitous slogan "BOAC takes good care of you." After the war, the policy was to hire accomplished, charming women interested in an exciting interim employment that would enhance the airline's image. The slogan was then augmented with promises of fine foods and "impeccable service." Jill belonged to a group of young women who had moved beyond the interim employment idea: she was a career stewardess.

So I made my way to the rear galley where she seemed to be involved, I thought somewhat aimlessly, in reshuffling pots and food containers.

She looked at me earnestly. "Dominic," she said, "how close was it?"

I wondered if I should make light of the situation, but I elected to be straight forward with a fellow crew member, "Jill we had less than five minutes. The tanks were dry!"

"Oh oh—"

I sensed she was disturbed. She had tasted the element of real danger that her career would entail. But for me it was very different; we had looked doom in the face and had stared it down. My sleeplessness, despite an interminable duty day, was due to a sense of elation.

Later in the day, BOAC flew in a replacement crew on a chartered eight-seat de Havilland Dove. I think we all felt a little cheated being mere passengers. Normally crew think of aircraft as types, only giving consideration to individuality when it come to maintenance records. In this case, I think we felt a kind of proprietary sense for the aircraft G-APDE and wanted to be the ones to see it back in regular operation. However, in the spirit of a good crewman, it was just another day's work!

CHAPTER NINETEEN

THE KINGDOM OF CEYLON

Sri Lanka was known to us as Ceylon when I made a number of trips to Colombo in 1959 and 1960. That was a time of violent political upheaval in Sri Lanka. As the unifying power of the colonialist administration declined, the various ethnic groups, including Sinhalese, Tamils, and Buddhists, clashed. 1958 saw riots in which thousands of the Tamil minority perished. In September 1959, the assassination of the Prime Minister, Bandaranaike, made world news headlines. He was succeeded in power by his widow, the first woman head of state. On the international political scene, the Sinhalese dallying with Communist politics caused difficulties with its traditional allies. The escalation of the disunity politics between Sinhalese and Tamils was to later lead to a prolonged murderous civil war, with terrorist and genocidal actions.

During our visits, we were aware that there were violent Buddhist demonstrations in downtown Colombo, and so were cautious when exploring the city. But these momentous events did not really enter our calculus. Amazingly, in our everyday dealings with people serenity and good will were abundant despite the uncontrolled violence in the offing. Our flying operations seemed to be unaffected.

Many of our passengers for Ceylon originated in or were bound for Colombo, which was serviced by two airports, one more primitive than the other. As one BOAC manager reported: "Jaffna Airport was primitive, and had no runway lights. so, whenever a Comet went through Colombo [Katunayika every night], they lit an old RAF kerosene gooseneck flare path, which took them over an hour. This was just in case of a diversion which happened only once or twice a year....[18]"

BOAC's preferred airport was naturally Katunayika. Even though from the air it looked like just a clearance in the jungle it was the best equipped, and only about one-hour ride to the city. If forced by a diversion due to weather to land at the Jaffna airport, passengers for Colombo could very well be subjected to a longer bus ride than their plane journey.

I first arrived in Katanayaka by Flight 791 from Hong Kong by way of Singapore on the 16 July 1959. On that trip, I was operating as E2 (flight engineer number two), meaning there were two qualified flight engineers on board, whereas only one was required for operations. This use of supernumerary crew is airline practice to ensure that technically competent crew are familiarized with the practical exigencies of route operations. For example, even senior captains will be assigned a "check" captain when working on a new route.

Coming from Hong Kong's Kai Tak airport, with its state of the art facilities, Katanayaka gave the impression of venturing into a different *era.* "Arrivals" was a dimly lit building that cried out wartime utility construction. Upon exiting customs and immigration, there was a room that housed the airline desks. Opposite these desks was a closet with a small counter in its doorway. On the counter sat a large aluminum teapot and cups. The tea growers' association of Ceylon dispensed splendid cups of tea from this most unassuming setup. I enjoyed their offering while the stewardess grimaced at, I am sure, she thought might be the unsanitary conditions. But I was reassured, knowing the infusion temperature for tea.

On that first flight, it was near 10:30 p.m. when the crew bus left the airport to take us to the Mount Lavinia Hotel. Since I had not been to the tropics before, I was astonished by the warm humid air at that time of the evening. The journey of about one and a half hours was also intriguing, as we made our way through a mysterious jungle like forest. As the coach sped along a dark road, the darkness was pierced sporadically by shafts of moon light through the dense overhead canopy of trees, and occasionally by the lights of human habitation in the distance.

The Mount Lavinia Hotel was an imposing structure with an interesting history. It sat on a promontory, its striking white façade looking out upon a wide strand and the azure blue of the Indian Ocean. During the war, it had served as a hospital. A short time before, in 1957, it was the location for shooting the film *Bridge on the River Kwai.*[19] The movie is fictional, but the local scenery represents that of the Thai river called Khwae, where the Empire of Japan built the infamous Burma Railroad using POW's and slave labor under inhuman conditions, after the Fall of Singapore in 1942.

The hotel was not air-conditioned. We understood the infrastructure was not capable of supplying the necessary power. The plentiful mosquitoes were vexing, and, at night, we slept under a mosquito net. The net was a canopy suspended from the ceiling, and when one retired for the night, the net was carefully tucked all around beneath the mattress. Then this safe space tent was carefully examined for mosquitoes or other unwanted insects. But the whole procedure being foreign to me, I still had to learn a valuable lesson! When I slept with my big toe resting against the net, I found the blood suckers could feast *through* the net, leaving me with a painful swollen toe in the morning.

The vagaries of crew scheduling allowed three- and four-day stopovers there. I know that some used that time to get a suntan that would be a remarkable fashion note in London at any time of the year. On occasion, we sunbathers on the warm sandy strand would be treated to the sight of a passing fisherman and his historic picturesque outrigger canoe. Another source of amusement and wonder, was in observing the procurement of fresh coconuts from the adjacent trees. The would-be harvester placed a loop of rope on his ankles. Then grasping the tree trunk with his hands, he would pull his legs upward. Then on transferring his weight to his bent legs his fettered ankles would be jammed by the rope into the tree trunk, allowing him to move his body upward. This climbing motion was repeated until the harvester had ascended the forty feet or more to the crown and the coconuts. Sliding down the tree trunk with the spoils was easier, but just as dangerous.

There was a bus service to downtown, so, an adventurous stewardess and I, took a bus trip to visit the zoo. There, after we paid the entrance fee, we were confronted by a cage with a large polar bear. His fur was spotlessly white, but his stance registered despair: the climate, undoubtedly approaching 100 degrees Fahrenheit 100 percent humidity, must have thoroughly confused the poor arctic animal. On another bus trip, I discovered the Catholic Church staffed by two Irish priests. They greeted their fellow Irishman like a long-lost brother. Besides the well appointed church downtown Colombo, the priests also said Sunday Masses at the "church" in the Mount Lavinia area. This consisted of a meticulously cared-for hut with no walls and a thatched roof. Its poor box was fastened to a structural pole; I debated, using foreign currency was illegal, then I stuffed into it the collection of notes that I would have taken to the Hong Kong money changers.

A group of us organized a trip to Kandy. This required an overnight stay there. Our tour guide had a large American saloon car and we piled in for an exciting trip to the mountains, and for some relief from the tropical heat at the ocean side. We were visiting a city famed for its sacred Buddhist sites, one of which was the most sacred Buddhist site in Ceylon (Sri Lanka)—the Temple of the Tooth. There, is preserved one of Buddha's teeth. The whole city was interesting and colorful but as a tourist, I must admit, I did not feel a sense of the sacred. A visit to the Kandy tea museum was promising. From the time I was a child I had averaged one or two cups of tea a day without giving any thought to its production. We listened with rapt attention to the details of the production cycle, and were treated to a *cuppa* at the conclusion of the tour.

The scenic mountains and the refreshing change of climate contributed to a very enjoyable and satisfying tour. One experience, lunch on our outward-bound journey, I was forced to remember for a long time. We were given to understand by our tour guide we would stop at the house that under colonial rule would have been the regional center of power. Now, the Englishman and his family had gone and his residence was converted into a native epicurean center. This was to be a one of a kind experience! Indeed ,there was lots of food and a large array of dishes. I remember now that despite the language difficulties, the waiters conveyed to us not to eat the spiced onions—they would be too spicy for the foreigner's digestion! Despite the waiters' solicitude I did indeed eat something too spicy for the foreigner's digestion, and suffered, not just heartburn, but an allergy to the spice for a long time.

Exiting the country through Kataniyka provided me with my most terrifying customs experience ever. On departure, I noticed, with some amusement, the agent flexing the walls of my BOAC standard issue suitcase. These suitcases were made of a thin wall, but really tough, fiberboard. Rumor had it that there had been trouble in Colombo with BOAC crews involved with gold smuggling, so I thought the agent will soon tire of his implausible search for a hidden compartment. However, any trace of humor in the situation evaporated when what appeared to be the customs supervisor approached me:

"Sir" he said, "we need to do a personal search"

I was shocked at this extraordinary turn of events, as no crew members were ever subjected to such an indignity. I tried to make sense of it, without any success.

 Without giving an outward sign of anxiety, I responded,

"That's OK, but I want a member of my crew with me."

"I'm sorry Sir, but by law, we cannot do a personal search if another person is present"

So I thought, it is to be a strip search, indeed the ignominy of an orifice search! And why? When they find nothing will they the need to justify their behavior by faking a find? I had better hold firm!

"I am sorry, I need a crew member with me"

He paused a moment, and said,

"In that case we have to send you back to Colombo." Then he turned an left for his office.

Prison in Colombo! The vision that entered my mind was that of the sticky climate and the bewildered polar bear I had seen in the zoo.

Another problem arose in my mind—the rest of the crew had left the customs hall, and since I was supernumerary the aircraft could operate without me. I doubted the captain would enter any protest. While I stood there thinking I had no options, the supervisor returned. I felt sure he would tell me of the arrangements for my return to Colombo and I had no idea how to react to that.

"Will you accept if local BOAC staff are present."

"Yes, of course."

"Come this way."

It crossed my mind that they had been offended by the racial implications of my demanding a crew member to be present. We go to a room and I stand defensively by the wall. Two others come in. The BOAC staff man stands by the entrance where he came in, all the while carefully looking into space. The second customs man makes a perfunctory body search, his hands moving over my uniform while the supervisor stands to one side. I sensed his reluctance, particularly as he got to my legs. He did not want to be there either! Four wordless men left the room, and I moved to close up my suitcase that still lay on the customs bench. Rushing out to the tarmac, I see the aircraft door still open. Surprisingly, even my suit case made it on the flight.

CHAPTER TWENTY

INDIA

I recall a landing, and being on baseleg (meaning we had one more ninety-degree turn before lining up on the runway,) when my ear phones continuously repeated, "dahdidit diditdah dahdah." I realize the beacon was sounding "DUM DUM, DUM DUM. This was the call sign for Calcutta's airport, and, of course, for those familiar with the grotesque aspect of fire arms, the name of a type of bullet designed to maximize body damage. The bullet is named because of its development there to halt the continued advance of wounded enemy soldiers who were ecstatic whirling dervishes. Like many places in the Middle East, both Dumdum Airport and Calcutta City have been renamed.

For those of us who wished to visit places different from our familiar routine, Calcutta was a bonanza for the eyes and ears. As our crew bus approached The Great Eastern Hotel it carefully avoided a beautiful, sacred cow that sat in the middle of the busy thoroughfare. The obviously well cared for animal had a striking blue coat and sat calmly chewing its cud; seemly completely unaware of its exalted status. The Great Eastern hotel was the epitome of colonial grandeur, with an imposing façade and a grand reception hall. It had fine restaurants, and was walking distance from the center of the city.

One morning, I awoke early, and busied myself with showering before going downstairs and, hopefully, joining some of the crew for breakfast. I could hear the buzz of city life, engines revving, squealing brakes, and car horns. Above the din and clatter, I could hear a distinctly Eastern experience—the public chanting of prayer. I wondered was it Muslim or Hindu? Curious to see what else might be involved, I peered out the window and could make out a figure in Indian garb across the street proclaiming for everyone in general, and loud enough to be heard specifically in my room. Since the words were meaningless to me, the chant was just part of the mysterious East, but the cadence eventually burst through my consciousness he was chanting an Our Father, ten Aves and a Glory Be—to my amazement and edification, The Rosary.

After breakfast one day, a small group of us took an exploratory walk. We must have stood out as tourists, as we aimlessly wandered the downtown area soaking in the ambience and observing the nature of the commerce that made up the daily lives of Calcuttans. We came across a small figure sitting on the ground, surrounded by papers, Here was a man conducting his business sitting on the sidewalk in the midst of pedestrians. Certainly a curiosity for us. I visualized him in London, seated in an office behind a mahogany desk. Here was a powerful example of the clash of cultural experiences. It turned out, that he had a business that would have no counterpart in the West.

Conscious of our interloper status, we continued sauntering past as we had done with the other things that had excited our curiosity.

However, his friendly greeting quickly brought us to a halt. Here was someone open, friendly, and content with life. He was interested in who we were, and listened to our story of why we were there. What did he do? He was a letter writer. Who were his clients? We had noticed the Indian Civil Service to be strongly bureaucratic when passing through airports, and based on that experience and the many languages in use, we thought there would obviously be a great need for his services. However, from our discussion, it was evident that a lot of his work involved personal matters and advice, so he was something of a counselor, as well as a functionary. We waved good bye, feeling good, and more strongly connected to Calcutta.

At that time, before the city had a Metro, there was an area near Chowringee Road and Chowringee Place where, as the shadows lengthened in the evening and businesses closed their doors, some of the poor homeless would congregate. This was the territory just then being patrolled by Mother Teresa; here she would find some *in extremis* and care for them.

This is where I had a hauntingly heartwarming experience of family dynamics. I walked slowly on the sidewalk in Chowringee Place, trying to comprehend *this* way of existence. Would it be possible within the culture I came from? The obvious answer was, that with the Irish weather, no. But I consoled myself, that with religion and Irish hospitality things would be different. I noticed a mother in the doorway of a Bank. She was busy with many things, one of which was putting her children to bed for their night's sleep. I will guess the children's ages as 10, 7, and 2. Now, the older ones were being very obedient; lying down on a blanket and being still as instructed. But the two-year old was unable to cooperate.

I slowed my pace, judging it not to be intrusive to pass by a little more slowly. I see the two older children gamely took over the mothering needs for Mama, amusing the little one and getting him to join them lying on their bed, shielding his little body with their own. This would normally have been just heartwarming, but in fact was also heart rending, since the bed was the thin blanket spread on the cold hard stone work of the doorstep.

I moved on. I tried to relate the experience I had to a bigger picture, and to the social work ideas and philosophy that Catherine and I had explored in New York. Faced with the beauty and absolute goodness of the children's faces I was reinforced in her rejection of *The Case for Modern Man*. It seemed to me, that relativism and reductionism offered absolutely no explanation for the children's behavior.

BOAC had stopovers for crew also in New Delhi and Bombay. In those places, I was surprised to learn that they had a connection with the Celts. This is how it began. Leaving New Delhi, I was on the tarmac for the preflight checking of the aircraft. The mechanic doing the refueling was under the wing with his hose attached and a paper and pencil in hand figuring out his loading instructions. I stopped and listened as he did arithmetic audibly. It sounded curiously familiar.

I waited until he completed his summation and said, "will you say one, two, three, four, five, six, seven, eight, nine, ten in the language you are using,"

He hesitated somewhat taken aback, and then smiling said, "*aon, dó, trí, cathair, cúig, sè, seacht, ocht, naoi, deich*" counting perfectly in Irish or Gaelic just as I had learned to in County Tipperary in the shadow of Slievemon.

We both had more pressing things to deal with, so my hurried explanation naturally did not register with him. My stream of consciousness turned first to the integrity of the outside the aircraft, and then on the flight deck to all instruments reading appropriately and controls set for the "start engines check." But my subconscious had received a jolt: there was in fact no compelling conflict of East versus West, all being of the same family there was no need for a "social contract."

In New Delhi, we stayed at the Ashoka Hotel, a showcase for Indian hospitality, with an address in the Diplomatic Enclave. We enjoyed the friendly staff who, among other things, made sure our letters from home were available. The swimming pool was a favorite spot, and very enjoyable, given the warn Delhi climate. The chlorine level was very high and hard on the skin if one stayed submerged too long; but we trusted the hotel management's judgment that this was necessary to be on the safe side. We were all too familiar with the unpleasant side of international travel where the "bugs" of any locale are hard on the digestion of travelers!

Delhi could be seen by paid tour or by public transportation. There was much to see in the city that was very interesting. But, for example, as with The Red Fort, which was impressive in size and had seen many dynasties pass, they were not memorable unless one was steeped in history. On a couple of occasions, I was part of a group that took a taxi to Agra. This was about three hours away if the rush hour was avoided; my recall of the rush hour in Delhi is automobiles inching forward in a sea of bicycle riders. At Agra, one was overwhelmed with the architecture of the Taj Mahal, even if fuzzy on its historical implications.

Our meals were supplied by the Ashoka; but outside of gathering at meal times, the crews liked to get together for a chat. This was best done by avoiding the high "diplomat" prices in the Ashoka bar. A enterprising Sikh, friendly with all the crews, would transport on his bicycle to us, six two-liter bottles of beer to lubricate our incestuous talk about flying and BOAC operations. The beer was a very reasonably priced light lager, and no one complained about a need for English "suds."

Bombay (now Mumbai) stopovers were memorable for the crowded streets, the mass of humanity. At all hours of the day, pedestrians, each it seemed with a pressing mission, crowded the sidewalks. Although we did not get to see it, we knew that the commuter trains had passengers who travelled clinging to the outsides of the carriages. We were housed in a downtown hotel whose name I do not remember, but our favorite restaurant was Gaylord's, it had an Indian menu compatible with international palates. It would later become an international chain.

Bombay is, of course, steeped in history. There were fascinating connections to both Apostolic times and Celtic traditions in nearby Kerala and Goa. My European mindset was challenged to note, that Saint Thomas the Apostle had brought Christianity to the area long before it spread to much of Europe. However, the length of time in stopovers did not provide an opportunity to satisfy our curiosity.

CHAPTER TWENTY-ONE

BRITISH CHINA

Hong Kong was still under British rule when we flew there. It was a bustling exciting city and urban area. Getting there, via Kai Tac Airport was also exciting for air crews, and for the passengers as well, if they had a window seat. Kai Tac was rated as one of the world's more dangerous airports and is now closed. However, I thought that the dramatic topography and technically demanding nature of landing and takeoff created an alertness on the part of crew, and thus eliminated that common source of error that arises from mere routine.

Cities, as everyone agrees, have personalities, but to describe these personalities requires an excursion into history, speculation, and personal introspection that in the end is not compelling. For some cities, we all agree, the doing of ordinary things there take on a special glow. Hong Kong, like Rome or San Francisco, besides being a sunny welcoming exciting place had such a special attraction for visitors. Having an English breakfast *there* was attractive. Many of our crews were faithful to having bangers and mash at the British club. Similarly, city transportation, taking the tram to Victoria Peak or the Star Ferry to Kowloon, had the aura of excitement.

Hong Kong was, as is well known, an exclusive shopping environment, and their money changers were unique. It was fascinating to empty one's pockets of the odd amounts of notes and coins we had picked up worldwide and watch the money changer swishing the beads of his abacus, before he handed over a sum in Hong Kong dollars. Many purchased the made-to-order suits, fashioned of the highest quality English materials; it may have been the level of service that was the favorable factor—twenty-four hours from measurement to fitting. I purchased a chronometer wristwatch before the advent of digital watches. The guaranteed chronometer time keeping of less than a one second variation in a month was based on an incredible mechanical self winding Swiss escape mechanism.

Visits to the border with China could be made in a one day trip. These were pleasant excursions, but the dominant emotion was in gazing across the border and contemplating a billion human beings denied our freedoms.

Kai Tac airport began as a grass strip used by the RAF. During World War Two the Japanese occupied Hong Kong and built concrete runways. Similar to the theme of the film *The Bridge on the River Kawi*, they used POW (prisoner of war) labor for construction. The tiny Crown Colony of Hong Kong had few options for land use, so after the war, the main runway was extended into Kowloon Bay using landfill. The lengthened runway was a finger of land long enough for Comet 4 operations.

This *airport in a bay* was a runway in a basin surrounded by rugged mountains. At the base of the mountains high-rise buildings crowded the airport perimeter. Depending on the winds, landings could be in either directions on the runway. The easiest landing was a Waglin straight-in approach. In that case, the Comet 4 could make a normal ILS landing by entering the basin through a gap in the hills and touchdown on the tip of the finger at the southern end of the runway. An overshoot would, of course, have to account for hills rising to 2,000 feet within six miles of the base of the finger. Due to prevailing winds, the more common landing was the Chung King approach. In this case, the Comet 4 aircraft entered the basin as before and descended to 800 feet over the city buildings near the base of the finger at the northern end of the runway. The humorous side of this was often uttered in remarks that those in the aircraft could see into family living rooms. Having positioned the aircraft accurately the next maneuver was to make a descending 180-degree right turn to touchdown at the base of the finger. I am sure that the barnstorming Charles Lindberg would have loved it!

As noted earlier, a remarkable feature of the turbojet was its wonderful increased reliability over piston engines. The Rolls Royce Avon Mark 524 engines that powered the Comet 4 proved to be trouble free. But it is an inescapable truth that any such mechanical equipment will be subject to random failures. One such failure happened on 20 May 1961. Flight 934 was on route from Rangoon to Hong Kong when I experienced engine compressor surge.

The basic principle of the jet engine is easily understood; its compressor sucks air in, energy is added to the air stream in the form of a kerosene type fuel, and the air is exhausted at an increased speed. Accelerating the mass of air to a higher speed results in a reactionary force that propels the aircraft forward. Our four Rolls Royce Avon engines did this so reliably, that generally aircrew could expect to never experience an engine failure throughout their career.

On the date in question, our aircraft departed Rangoon at 05:39 a.m. Engine power was normal on takeoff and climb out. Before reaching TOC we experienced compressor stall. Now an Avon engine throttle, is a complex system, a computer, for managing the smooth flow of air through the engine. It allows changes in fuel flow, engine RPM, and thrust without compressor surge or stalls. A stall, if allowed persist is capable of great damage—of vibrations capable of breaking rotating parts. The worst-case scenario would be, an engine breaks even a single blade and due to the high rotational speed, enters into an engine wreaking vibration, leading to an uncontained engine failure. It is true that the Comet 4 engines were provided with protective armor to impede broken parts that could be flung outward, but how effective that armor would be was open to question. An uncontained failure in a Comet would be more destructive than that which occurred later in United Airlines Flight 232.[20] They lost their number two engine and damaged the tail plane, but in the Comet the engines were amidships and buried in the wings where the high energy debris would damage the adjoining engine, the fuel tanks, and the pressurized passenger cabin.

The symptoms we encountered, were a cyclic yawing of the aircraft, accompanied by a banging noise as the stalls occurred. Our instruments showed the fluctuations to be in the number four (starboard outer) engine. We throttled the engine back and advanced it to power again with a reoccurrence of the engine stalls. To continue would have resulted in mechanical damage. At that, as I suggested, we shut it down, and we completed our flight on three engines.

We arrived in Hong Kong at 10:54 a.m. A visual inspection of the number four engine did not reveal anything out of place. The engine also started and ran normally at idle, where, in fact, stalls most often occur. It seemed that the fault had to do with engine control under conditions of flying at altitude, something that could not be replicated on the tarmac in Hong Kong. Given the seriousness of the malfunction it was concluded that unless there was a positive identification of the problem the engine should be removed. In later follow up, I learned that in manufacture there was a miss-assembly of the entry guide vanes. These control the intake air and respond to multiple conditions when flying at cruise speeds.

CHAPTER TWENTY-TWO

THE LAND OF THE RISING SUN

Beyond the Middle East our Comet 4 routes extended to Tokyo. It is interesting that the most common code name for Japan, "Land of the Rising Sun," is a statement of a Chinese perspective. It also conveys a sense of the remoteness of Japan. From a Western perspective. Francis Xavier arrived there in 1549, but it was to be three hundred years before the West could be said to engage commercially with Japan. In 1853 the American, Commodore Perry, opened Japan to Western trade. When I arrived, Tokyo was a city of modern developments, skyscrapers, department stores, and public transit. While these dissipated some of the mysteries of the Land of the Rising Sun, Tokyo differed from the other cities where we had crew stopovers—it was not related to the British colonial traditions. Thus in Hong Kong, Rangoon, Singapore, Calcutta, New Delhi, Bombay,

Colombo, Kuala Lumpur, and Karachi the elements foreign to us were muted by a long=standing British presence.

I first flew into Tokyo on the 9 February 1960. It had been one hundred years since Commodore Perry's arrival, and just fifteen years since the end of World War Two. It was puzzling how a history of a closed feudal society, an opening to Western commerce, the unspeakable brutalities of the Japanese war of conquest by the Empire of Japan, and an American occupation, had resulted in what I experienced—polite, friendly, and gracious Japanese allies. One quickly learned that the basic words in any transaction were *arigatou* (thanks) and *arigatou gozaimasu* (thanks very much).

Our stopovers in Tokyo, due to the distinctiveness of the society, had a strong tourist flavor. People were dissimilar from *us* in appearance and stature, and unlike the Middle East and India the English language was no help in communications. I was abruptly reminded of the question of stature early on. Having newly arrived, I had not yet ventured beyond our hotel at lunch time. In the basement, I found a cozy café with English translations in the menu, and was directed to my table by the gracious hostess. So far so good. I observed before sitting down that the chair and table were constructed for a smaller frame than mine. I sat down and pushed my knees under the table, except that my knees did not go *under* the table; rather they impacted the table top support apron, sending all the cutlery and china crashing to the floor. I am not sure whether I or the bevy of waitresses that arrived to help, were the most embarrassed.

In Tokyo, our BOAC crews routinely got together for dinner at some recommended restaurant or club. This left the daytime open for individual exploration. With tourist literature and knowledge of a small number of Kanji characters, such as those for "in" and "out," it was possible to explore the city. It was exciting to wander through the open-air market and other public places. On trips to department stores, I found household items of unique Japanese design, to the great delight of Catherine and myself, who at that time were engrossed in thoughts of housekeeping together. In these transactions, I was enchanted by the warm helpful nature of the person-to-person exchanges; and that culture, history, and language were only minor obstacles. In the open-air food market, I eyed the *raw* fish delicacies with apprehension, and immediately the vendors offered to freely give them to me, just to see the foreigner appreciate them. How did I know the vendors intent? There was no mistaking the conviviality and body language.

Travel around the city had a sense of adventure and satisfaction, but one stewardess, not content to come 10,000 miles and just tour a big city, had a more ambitious idea. A single female travelling alone would be problematic so she asked if I would make a day trip to the seaside. She, armed with tourist literature and maps, and I, armed with a little red phrase book that had a pronunciation guide and Kanji characters, started early in the morning.

We negotiated the city transport to the interurban train station. There we purchased the return tickets for a forty-five- minute ride. Once aboard the train, we became concerned about recognizing where to get off, and anxiously scanned each station board. With relief, we found our destination station, but now we were challenged to find the beach we wished to add to our touristic accomplishments. I thought, "a taxi—a taxi driver will be the most accomplished person to deal with foreigners." But where was the taxi rank?

I turned to a friendly looking fellow, and using my little red book, I attempted the pronunciation given—only to be met with a baffled look. I was, of course, prepared for that, so I showed him the Kanji character—this time to be met with a pained look of incomprehension. Turning to my companion I said, "oh we may never get a taxi."

"Ah," the fellow shouted with glee, "Taxi."

He gestured across the parking lot with a flourish, and in a moment, with smiles all around, we were climbing into our taxi.

But now there was "beach." Again, there were the muttered pronunciations and Kanji characters, but they seemed to work well this time. Our taxi sped off, and in a minute or two pulled into a semicircular driveway to an imposing building. On the sidewalk, was a long line of maids spaced out with military precision. They were dressed European style, wearing black dresses with white collars, gloves, aprons, and headpieces. A doorman opened the taxi door.

Utterly confused about my next move, I paid the taxi and climbed out, followed by my companion. As we passed each maid, she joined her hands in a prayerful gesture and bowed from the waist. In a dazed fashion, we passed the line of maids, and walked past the entrance door; carefully not making eye contact with the small knot of men standing there. My companion was obviously looking to me for leadership, so I continued round the driveway and onto the street, anxious to place distance between us and the "hotel."

When safely away from the scene of our embarrassment, we stopped to review the situation. We were completely puzzled by where we had been, and had no theories about the "royal" reception. Using her map, we plotted a dead-reckoning course for the beach, and surprisingly enough, succeeded. But what a surprise! There were no sun worshipers, no little children with sand pails; as far as the eye could see the sand stretched out with no human forms visible.

Our faith in the taxi driver brotherhood being shattered, we did our sightseeing by walking; getting back to the interurban train station for the afternoon train to the city. This time, we were heading to the terminus, so there was no worry about where to get off. Across the aisle in the train sat three men easily identified by their garb as businessmen. As we rode on to the terminus, they produced a bottle of Scotch whiskey that they shared by filling a jigger and, taking turns, quaffing it down. They beckoned to us too, and we thought it a suitable adventure, but the language barrier was too high.

CHAPTER TWENTY-THREE

A SUCCESSFUL COLONY

I t was as recent as the year 1818, when Sir Thomas Stamford Raffles arrived in the small fishing village, Singapore. It was his intent to found a British trading post and a free port, to challenge the Dutch monopoly of commerce in the East Indies. Bordering as it does the Straits of Malacca, that is sometimes termed "the world's most important trade route," the village grew, with an influx of Chinese, Malays, Indian, and Europeans attracted by the profitable entrepôt trading. As it grew in size and influence, these groups did not form a unity, but lived in separate racial enclaves. The Chinese enclave was further subdivided by region, Cantonese and so on. During the nineteenth-century Singapore grew to became an impregnable fortress, a vital part of the British Empire.

Singapore Island is one degree of latitude north of the equator, with a tropical rainforest climate. Weather is not seasonal, so light clothing and an umbrella should be sufficient to set the visitor at ease. Central to our aircraft operations was the fact that, similar to the Caribbean, the area is rich in thunderstorms. At that latitude these very dangerous, majestic storms reached higher than our absolute 44,000-foot ceiling. In daylight, while we threaded our way around them to avoid the large hail, icing, up and down draughts, and the extreme turbulence they contained, they appeared as colossal, dark, menacing sentinels. At nighttime, when they were unseen, we gave heartfelt thanks for our weather radar that clearly painted their dense watery cores.

With BOAC's large number of flights through Singapore, there was always a flight leaving shortly after our rest period ended. So, stopovers in Singapore were short, but there was still time for exploration. Like most visitors, we savored the experience of exploring and bargaining in the world-famous Tin Pan Alley. It was here that *caveat emptor* reigned supreme, and for us typified what we Westerners thought to be the Oriental approach to trading. With any of the small independent merchants there, it could be you bargained hard and paid only one quarter of the asking price, and still paid more than you needed to. It was great fun to wander and see the huge eclectic collection of products at bargain prices. My firm resolution to be just a window shopper was overcome when I saw a multimeter (amps, ohms, volts meter) at an unbelievably good price. I held strongly to my fifty percent offer for it, and walked away with the instrument, that gave good service until outdated by the digital revolution many years later. Beyond Tin Pan Alley there was also a very lively trade in jewelry and luxury goods, which I, merely assumed, to be at attractive prices.

Dining out was an adventure. Though my personal favorite was Indonesian Fried Rice, *Nasi Goreng,* I very much enjoyed Chinatown, where there were restaurants that functioned in a way uniquely suitable to the local circumstances of unvarying weather, warm climate, wok cooking, Chinese spices, and Chinese business acumen. Typically, these restaurants had outdoors, at each side of the entrance doorway, two lively fires with flames licking the undersides of huge woks that gave off mouth watering odors. At the doorway, each customer gave his order from the menu. This was recorded by the maitre d' but the cook would be adding ingredients to the wok as the conversation preceded. Each meal occupied a unique moving space on the wok, sequencing through different heat zones. After the customer was comfortably seated in the air-conditioned interior his sizzling hot meal quickly arrived.

A favorite recreational spot was the Raffles Hotel, noted for its long history, colonial pride, and the literary figures who had stayed there. Dining within its ambience was akin to joining in the excitement and freedom of being part of a fiction novel. It is named for the founder of the colony, and has participated significantly in all the episodes of its history, but it is even more prominently featured in fiction. The hotel had associations with luminaries like Noel Coward, Somerset Maugham and Rudyard Kipling.

Often our arrivals and departures in Singapore came with the short hop to or from Kuala Lumpur. The airport there featured a railway embankment a short distance from the end of the runway. Though this was not as complex as the situation at Kai Tac Airport in Hong Kong, it did color our thinking about operations there. I recall on one occasion, as we entered the Kuala Lumpur runway the captain called for takeoff power. As I watched the pilots' hands on the throttles I observed the RPM and JPT gauges on the center panel up front. Then a quick look at the fuel flow meters on my engineer's panel confirmed that the starboard outer (number four) engine had not come up to power. We had started our takeoff roll, but the ever-present phrase "full power four engines" died in my throat, and I called, "engine failure." The call elicited a smooth response from the front. The captain said, "abort," and pulled the throttles back to "idle." He braked and steered left at the runway exit, while the first officer calls on the radio for permission to return to the gate. An engine failure on takeoff is always a very critical event, but we had been in little danger. The failure was well before V1, and the aircraft was lightly loaded for the hop to Singapore. Still, we were pleased with our performance, and that indefinable, seamless, crew coherence.

Many of our BOAC crew members were very conscious of the more recent history of The Battle of Singapore, and the three-year Empire of Japan occupation during World War Two, with its humiliations and brutalities. As we have noted, the general outlook worldwide after the war tended to be positive and hopeful for a new age; but senior crew members had associations with the RAF, and were forcefully confronted with the pivotal role the destruction of the RAF played in the calamitous defeat seventeen years earlier. Beyond the Singapore Military High Command's conceptual errors, such as complacency, overconfidence, the mistaken judgment about the impenetrability of the jungle invasion route, and racial misconceptions about the war hardened Japanese soldiery, there was a strategic error in equipping the air forces with the inferior Brewster Buffalo fighter aircraft. There are legions of stories about the inadequacies and lack of performance of these, that some pilots referred to as "flying coffins."

With the start of Japanese hostilities, Allied air power was quickly wiped out through combat, destruction on the ground, and accidental mishaps. At sea, the Allied warships, without air support, fell easy prey to the Japanese aircraft torpedoes. On the ground, there was practically no protection from Japanese bombing of cities and strategic assets. Without close-in air support the Allied infantry, though superior in numbers, were soundly defeated. To quote an Army officer, "the British

Empire came to an end in 1997, but more importantly the *beginning of the end* of the British Empire was at the Fall of Singapore." This dismal history oppressed some of our crew.

However, in the 1960s, Singaporeans were engaged in rebuilding the good life. We could see physical evidence of their success; "as far as the eye could see," the Singapore straits had ships at anchor. Their multi-ethnic population moved to transform their colony into a nation.

CHAPTER TWENTY-FOUR

VENTURING DOWN UNDER

Many Europeans have emotional ties to Australia. The Irish had revered national revolutionary heroes who were transported to the penal colony there. As well as that, many had family who emigrated to Australia seeking a better life. The year 1848, poetically known as "Springtime of the Peoples," was a year of revolutions and agitation for universal suffrage throughout Europe. In Ireland, those nationalists opposed to Daniel O'Connell and his putsch for federalization—Irish independence within the British system—were known as Young Irelanders. The name was obviously influenced by the ideals of Giuseppe Mazzini and *La Giovine Italia*. The village in County Tipperary where I grew up, saw the culmination of the Young Irelanders movement. Indeed, by an amazing coincidence the bedroom I slept in as a young boy was the meeting place where they held their final war council in 1848.

In that room, a group of about fifteen intellectually high-minded patriots debated the weighty questions: if armed rebellion was by then *inevitable,* or, in fact, *impossible* with a ragtag army of famine afflicted people, already *dying* daily of starvation. After that war council, many of the participants were captured and sentenced to death. But they had their sentences commuted, since reputedly, Queen Victoria intervened, and they were, instead, sent to Van Diemen's Land (Tasmania); But these were men of heroic stature, and eventually one served as Governor of Queensland, Australia; another as Governor of Montana in the USA. Others had roles in the American Civil War, and they planted the seeds of Irish republicanism for the twentieth century.

Apart from these heroic connections, a flavor of family attachments, and how families were dispersed over Ireland, England, Australia, Canada, and the United States can be seen in a four-page letter from my Grandfather to his Australian cousin in 1924. Thomas' first cousin, John Barrett, eleven years his senior was born and raised in County Tipperary, but moved first to London, England and then to Australia *circa* 1870. Thomas Wall writes:

The Commons
Slievardagh. Thurles
Co. Tipperary
May 15th, 1924

My Dear Cousin
I received your letter all right. To say I was surprised,
would be to put it very mildly. I was simply
thunderstruck after all those nigh countless years
you were living strongly and well beneath the Land of
the Southern Cross or Sunny Australia without I ever
having a single line from you since you left London for
your adopted country. But however, all is well that ends
well. I was more than delighted I assure you to learn
that you were still going strong, and was occupied with
an ardent desire to visit the Old Country again. If you
do a "caed mile failte" will await you here, as anything
we can do will be at your disposal. I am now living....

Thomas goes on to recount births, deaths, and other incidents of
interest in three continents in the previous fifty-four years. What can
be clearly seen is the unifying effect of kinship and language, despite
differences in dialect, nationality, and religion. With this background, I
looked forward with curiosity to meeting Australians and visiting Down
Under.

In 1960, BOAC's route—London, England to Melbourne Australia—
was the longest airline route in the world. Prior to the opening of the
Suez Canal in 1869, you could have made that trip on a fast Clipper ship

in about three months, sailing around the Cape of Good Hope in South Africa. To avoid strong, westerly trade winds south of the Cape of Good Hope, your return adventure, would undoubtedly have you sail home by Cape Horn in South America; thus, circumnavigating the globe. The opening of the Suez canal shortened the journey. But sailing vessels could not *sail* through the canal and a further technological invention was needed to make that route practical for steamships. The invention of the more efficient compound steam engine made it possible to carry sufficient coal. In this way, the time for a surface journey to Australia was halved. The Comet 4 made the trip in ten sectors of approximately three hours each. So, given the flying time and the transit times at each sector as well as the time zone changes, passengers departing London at noon on Monday could expect to greet their friends about noon on Wednesday in Melbourne. The time zones would make the return trip seem short, since the passengers leaving Melbourne at noon on Monday could expect to greet theirs London friends about 4:00 p.m. on Tuesday. The jetliner was shrinking the world!

Due to flight time limitations (FTL) airline crews would have had five stopovers on the outward-bound trip from London to Australia and five more on the return. It was inevitable that our final stopover before Australia was at Singapore.

My first flight to Australia was in December 1959. The final legs of the trip begun with the departure of Flight 714 from Singapore at 8:25 p.m. for Jakarta. Jakarta was not a scheduled stop but, depending on the headwinds to be encountered, the aircraft would be refueled there for the long haul to Darwin and the fuel for an alternate if such became necessary. Shortly after leaving Singapore International Airport at Paya Lebar (now closed), which is at 1.3 degrees north latitude, the equator is crossed. Even though it is only an imaginary line drawn around the earth, there is a sense of achievement in reaching latitude 0°. This sentiment is common and the moment of passing from the northern to the southern hemisphere and now being "down under," is always of interest to crew and passengers.

We refueled at Jakarta Airport (later closed), and on leaving in the darkness we had, according to our flight plan, four hours and five minutes to traverse approximately 1,700 miles. On the flight deck, every knob and instrument face was familiar and all were behaving as expected. But to assume everything was under control would degrade vigilance. To actively keep one's self in the right mindset—situational awareness—demanded a comprehensive picture of the world. Our flight plan would take us over an Indonesian archipelago of tropical islands and over the open Timor Sea. I mentally checked—had I the Air Ministry pamphlet on jungle survival in my briefcase? Yes! Would our track be safely far to the west of the cannibalistic tribes of Papua? Yes! Although we were not to know about it until later; that was the place where the Harvard-Peabody Expedition would be conducted in 1961–1963, and where Michael Rockefeller may have been eaten by cannibals.

The remoteness and lack of airports suitable for Comet 4 operations was a concern. I am sure Captain Kemp was thinking of the many landing strips built by the military in the war with the Empire of Japan that ended just fourteen years earlier. They would be unsuitable for normal operations, but aircrews like to know what their options are should the unexpected happen. As we hoped, the flight was uneventful, and we flew on to Darwin arriving at 5:20 a.m. before sunrise on the 15th of December in the Australian monsoon season of 1959.

Darwin is a center of population in Australia's sub-tropical wilderness and the capitol of Northern Territories. However, its most undesirable claim to exclusivity may be, that it was the "Australian Pearl Harbor," and had been repeatedly bombed by the Japanese in the recent war in sixty-four raids against the Darwin area. After the unexpected raids, a large part of the population fled the city; the territory was placed under military control. By 1959 people had returned, and the city had been rebuilt. The outpost in a harsh territory had been given a city charter.

During our stopovers, we stayed at the Fannie Bay Motel, a short distance from the city center. Unlike the Mount Lavinia Hotel in Ceylon, it was air-conditioned. It was equipped with window air-conditioners that excited my curiosity because they had a heating mode selector. I wondered, "was it possible that this incredibly hot sticky climate ever got cool enough that you would turn the switch to that selection?" Beyond the enervating weather, the dense clouds of insects in the afternoons made the exploration of the outside a challenge. I took the challenge, and headed north on the road from the hotel with the Fannie Bay on my left. My curious gaze caught sight of a large brown animal loping along in the field to my right. To my utter delight, I had encountered my first marsupial; a big brown wallaby. Regretfully, before I could gather my thoughts to study the animal's gait it loped over the hillock with amazing rapidity.

To attend Sunday Mass, I consulted the information provided by the motel, and called a taxi. I was more than curious to see a large group of Aboriginals in attendance at Mass. My boyhood adventures in County Tipperary were an exploration of a two-dimensional cosmos. Here in Darwin was an escapade in time, a 40,000-year-old culture; that was already ancient before the age of empires. The aboriginal people could as well be from a distant planet, for their lives, culture, and psychology were that distant from ours.

Just as a visit from non-terrestrials would, their presence raised profound questions, particularly about existence and justice—what does it mean to be human and how should we treat others? These are the questions that particularly arise when civilizations meet primitive tribes. This was the problem that faced the Spanish in the New World, some 300 years before the English settlers arrived in Australia. The Spanish questioned whether the natives had the human dignity to be Christians. The culmination of that controversy came when the King Charles V of Spain issued the *Layes Nuevas* (New Laws) in 1542. These declared that the aboriginals were indeed children of God and, as citizens of the empire, were not to be enslaved. Of course, despite the best efforts of the Dominican clergy the New Laws were not implemented perfectly but, it is interesting to note, they did establish valuable precedents and principles that had to be established *de novo* in Australia.

When, the first visitors, the Dutch sailors made land fall in what they called, *Terra Australis Incognita* in the early 1660s, and saw the bipedal, language talking aboriginal people, they had no trouble knowing they were human. However, whether for genuine or self-serving reasons in later interactions settlers questioned if they had the proper *interior life* of humans. They recognized the Australian Aboriginals shared with them and other animals the interior life of the senses, imagination, memory, and emotions, but questioned did they have the higher elements of the interior life of humans; concepts of universals, the existential awareness and judgments of self, nature, and the supernatural. If they lacked any aspect of this higher faculty they would be subhuman, incapable of property rights, of self governance, and killing them would not be murder. Some of the early actions of settlers leaned to such an interpretation. The government proclaimed that they had no ownership of land and, particularly in Tasmania where tribal warfare erupted, they were killed without qualms and with legal immunity. It was, however, very evident that their interior life was suffused with religious sentiment and their individuality and humanity unquestionable. After the Tasmanian events, there were no major attempts to eliminate the Aboriginals. Rather there were practical problems.[21]

The 1700s and 1800s had no lack of theories, scientific research, political ideologies, and pseudo-scientific theories, such as phrenology and eugenics, that could influence the actions of individuals or institutions. However, the practical problems were paramount. It had to be faced that the hunter-gatherer lifestyle was no longer possible. But more than that, the Aboriginal lifestyle was in many respects intolerable. For example, there was the tit-for-tat revenge cycles of tribal violence, and forms of child abuse, as well as exposure to diseases. The bishop of Darwin was called, "the bishop of 150 wives" because he bought so many young girls to set them free to marry their person of choice and prevent their forced sale to old men. To lead productive and peaceful lives Aborigines would need concepts of natural law, particularly private property rights and a civic identity.

What was needed could not be negotiated by a strictly secular state. Australia was secular, it disestablished the Church of England in 1836 and offered free secular compulsory education in 1850. Such a state would have a form of fairness as its final end that implied only that un-coerced parties agree freely.[22] But the Aborigines would not succeed in such a confrontation; what was needed for justice was an empathetic, *loving* intervention. The loving intervention could only be supplied by those with a higher final end than that of the secular society. Elementary justice had to wait for a new approach.[23]

It was encouraging to observe the black parishioners' pious participation in the service but I noted they all sat together on one side of the church. After Mass, the priest processed out and stood outside to greet us.

After the small talk, I asked, "Father, why are the aboriginals segregated?"

"Oh," he smiled, "they prefer it that way, they like to sit together."

I became dimly aware as I watched the Aboriginal congregation at Mass, that the cherished symbols of my boyhood—separation of spiritual and civic powers, democracy, and freedom—needed to add another one—the *cooperation* of spiritual and secular powers.

I also undertook to explore downtown Darwin by walking there. This was an exhausting three-mile journey and I doubted my sanity after I had undertaken it. However, after starting there was no turning back. The scenery brought to mind the secluded walled compounds I had seen in Bahrain when I saw there the very antithesis of that. I observed the way in which many houses were placed seemingly at random on stilts in the fields. In the unfenced open space underneath them were the machines and equipment of daily life. I understood the practicality of raising the living spaces, since in the afternoons in open spaces at ground level, there was that intense fog of insects. These flying insects, except for the mosquitoes, did not appear to be bothersome. In my state of exhaustion, downtown was not exciting. But before calling a taxi, I tried to "drink in" the local scene by ordering a cooling milkshake in an ice cream parlor that had attracted a crowd of young people. The milkshake had a strong flavor of dried milk!

Some crew members who were possessed of an exploratory curiosity like mine, had met with our friendly neighbors near the hotel. One neighbor confirmed for them the primitive, harsh nature of the place by taking them to see his *pet* crocodile that he confined in a tub.

In the evening, at the crew socializing in the motel bar, I was surprised to see the hotel served beer in stemmed wine glasses! The explanation that the smaller quantities could be kept colder in the tropical climate rang hollow in the air-conditioned bar. This is a fashion that was also much debated as to whether it inhibited or contributed to alcohol abuse. I had another culinary surprise in the morning, when I ordered the very reasonably priced steak and eggs. The steak was the toughest meat I ever had.

The explanation for the toughness of the meat was, I learned, the vastness of the range on which the beef was raised. The Australian cowboy in the huge stations (ranches) in the Northern Territory employed a helicopter, not on a horse. The vastness and emptiness of Australia was made evident to us in the flight sectors between Darwin and Sydney. Depending on the winds aloft the flight time was between four and five hours, and throughout the trips only Alice Springs showed the signs of human occupation.

Our stopovers were in Melbourne. This city was noted for its many similarities to San Francisco, California in its climate, hilly terrain, and cable cars. I would have liked to explore this *urban* Australia, but our time in town was too short.

Airlines have a form of organization dictated by the nature of their operations. Primarily for safety reasons, operations and maintenance operate at arm's length and not, as might be expected, in a traditional pyramidal structure. Flight crew have, of course, an interest in safety as well as in on-time operation. The different perspectives come into play with transit times, that is the period from the arrival of the aircraft to its departure. Many passengers will have experienced the practical effects of it. When a delay occurs because of equipment failures the operations staff are often evasive; because they seem to work for a *different* organization and they, too, are in the dark.

Transit times are largely outside the control of the flight crew. But, as to be expected, the flight engineer kept a proprietary eye on all that was happening on the tarmac. On transits where no passengers are deplaned or boarded, such as those we had in Gander, Canada, the time is determined solely by the time to upload fuel. A normal time with passengers deplaning and uploading was about one hour.

We had concerns about the language difficulties and culture of ground staff in the Middle East and Far East. In Australia, there was no language barrier, and we had a high level of confidence in the services of those we might indeed claim as distant cousins. However, in World War Two, their soldiers were credited with being insubordinate, fearless, no-nonsense, and assertive so we expected them to be confrontational. The airline structure together with what we called "Aussie attitude" created a hyper-professional atmosphere in some cases.

One transit in Sydney that was atypical, but illustrative of the edginess that can occur. On the tarmac, I checked among many things the fuel hoses had been removed, the fuel access panels closed, the cargo hatches locked, the passengers boarded, and the transit time about an hour, Now I thought, where was the station engineer? He had taken the aircraft logbook from its normal place on the flight deck and placed it on a trolley with various papers and equipment. I looked at the logbook and it seemed in order, so I put it back on the flight deck.

In a couple of minutes, while I was checking the configuration for taxiing he appeared on the flight deck,

He inquired loudely, "Who took the logbook?"

I said, "It's here, we need to get moving."

"Did you know you can't move the aircraft without my signature?"

"Here is the book!"

He signed the logbook, and we left on time.

CHAPTER TWENTY-FIVE

SOUTH AMERICA

On the ocean that hollows the rocks where ye dwell,
A shadowy land has appeared, as they tell;
Men thought it a region of sunshine and rest,
And they called it Hy-Brasail, the isle of the blest;
From year unto year, on the ocean's blue rim,
The beautiful spectre showed lovely and dim;
The golden clouds curtained the deep where it lay,
And it looked like an Eden, away, far away![24]

This was the first of four verses, in our primary school reader, of Gerald Griffin's poem about the most intriguing of the legendary islands off the coast of Ireland. Whether the island of Irish mythology influenced the name of South America's largest state is lost in antiquity; but we liked to think it did.

Hy-Brasail is part of the Celtic mythology of heroic journeys to strange lands where people did not age, were always happy, listened to ethereal music, and were un-afflicted by illnesses—not heaven in the afterlife, but heaven on earth. The Land of Promise, *Tir na Og* (Land of Youth) fired the imagination of all of us young would-be explorers. The storied island expressed so well the excitement, the wonder, and discovery of travel. This island was shown on British Admiralty charts into the nineteenth century, but Christopher Columbus and John Cabot were looking for a passage to India, so they were not concerned about *Hy-Brasil's* physical presence. They were undoubtedly influenced by its symbolic and historical aspects. So too with us youthful scholars in Tipperary, we accepted it was mythical, not physical, but we were attuned to its mystical aspects. So I can say, that the excitement I felt at 05:40 hours on 18 November 1960, as we departed Daker in Africa for Recife, Brazil owed something to Gerald Griffin.

On our South American trips, we had stopovers in Rio de Janeiro, São Paulo in Brazil, and in Santiago, Chile. The time spent in Rio de Janeiro had a festive air and the crews made the visits to the attractions: Copacabana and Ipanema beaches, the cable car ride to Sugarloaf Mountain, with its iconic Christ the Redeemer monument atop Corcovado. It was rumored that a tour of a *favela* was possible but I elected to see them from a distance. They could be hazardous in a number of ways, they lacked sanitation, failed to follow building codes, and were known to be crime-ridden. At that time, the government was making a determined effort to wipe them out, and some had been eliminated. Even from a distance the hodgepodge construction excited sympathy for the dwellers and instilled caution in a potential visitor. In contrast, the city streets exuded an air of wealth and civic order. Walking the Portuguese-style cobblestone pavements was, in itself, enjoyable, where the distinctive patterns or illustrations of each section was the creation of individual artists. I was struck by the friendliness and outgoing character of city. A hesitant request for directions was invariably met with a fulsome response.

There was a story shared among the crews that warned of a form of larceny, possibly unique in the whole world to Copacabana beach. It could befall the unwary naïve sunbather. The victims were never identified in the telling, but the story goes something like this:

A BOAC fellow, armed with the expensive towels provided by our luxury hotel, hailed a taxi for the short ride to the beach. Once there he hunted for a suitable sunbathing spot. The sun worshippers and their children displayed a territorial instinct by creating towel walls and mounds in the deep sands to define their temporary ownership of a place in the sun. Our hero claimed his secluded spot in this undulating landscape where his possession was not challenged. There he could stretch out clothed only in his swim suit and sunglasses, and with his valuables close by. He could now relax and contemplate obtaining a tan that would be awesome in winter-shrouded England, surely a compensation in full for any trials that his career in aviation imposed.

On opening his eyes, he sees that his territorial boundaries have been breached by a friendly young lady of delectable proportions. She, overcoming whatever language difficulties there were, engaged him and convinced him to remove his swim suit. Instantly, she and companions, who unexpectedly appeared, walk away with his swim suit and all his other belongings. He had lost his money, papers, wallet, towels, watch. sunglasses, clothes; but worse still, it becomes clear to him as it did to Adam and Eve after they sinned—he was naked! Any thought of pursuit was impossible. He was imprisoned by an impenetrable wall of shame. He was not a deeply religious man, so any consideration of the original human experience of this problem was overpowered by the thought "I'm a bloody fool. The whole world will know I'm a bloody fool."

After cowering helplessly for a time, he was assisted by some kindly neighbors. They provided him with clothing and the essential taxi back to the hotel.

On one of my stays in Rio, I booked a tour, with a return flight, to Brasilia. This was the new state capitol that had been inaugurated just months earlier, and still had many elements under construction. The scope of the concept to unify the ancient states, and to colonize the vast territories of the Interior, was striking. President Kubitschek characterized it as "dawn of a new day for Brazil." What was planned was more than a federal capitol, Brasília was to be an administrative region similar to Washington D.C. In the day tour, we were introduced to the unique modernist architecture and the *avant garde* urban planning.

Our tour guide showed the daring architecture and purpose-built sections that would house the president, legislators, supreme court, diplomats and others. The plans were so detailed that even the color of the bus drivers' uniforms were specified. Rio de Janeiro and San Paulo were noted for their distinctive architecture; but here Brazilian architecture was to burst the bonds of concerns for human habitation to become concerns on a grander scale for *human living*. The tour guide described Vila Amaury, a separate city nearby that housed the construction crews, which we did not get to see. It was a stark contrast, a rough frontier town, and they planned to bury it at the bottom of a huge artificial lake when Brasilia was built.

I had misgivings; our flight deck was the ultimate in planned activity and yet situational awareness, handling the unplanned activities that arose, was the most important part of the work. I wondered if the hyper-planning would be an obstacle to the development of the Federal District? The spectacular city when completed was widely acclaimed. It opened up the central area of Brazil and attracted development away from the crowded southeast. It was chosen by UNESCO as a World Heritage Site. But the planners expected even more—a modern utopia. Their excessive expectations expressed in the conceit that the lifeless flowing lines made possible through the twentieth-century technology of reinforced concrete construction were described as *womanly*. But the elitist planning, like the socialistic five-year plans very popular in other countries at that time, succumbed to organic development as the city attracted more and more residents.

In flying to São Paulo, I came to an appreciation of the thrill of discovery that Columbus must have felt at the sight of Hispaniola. He knew the world was round, so he was certain there was land ahead, but it was only with the shout, *"terra a vista"* that his theoretical knowledge was augmented with the actuality of the place. I knew of the large cities in South America. I had seen pictures of the sights of Rio de Janeiro. But the existence of the bustling metropolis of São Paulo was a surprise to me. It was the largest city we visited and was famous for the diversity of its population. As one proud resident told me, it had the largest Japanese community outside of Japan. When I arrived there in November 1960, I astonished that I could know so little of the actuality of South America.

São Paulo celebrates its antiquity and modernist architecture. Given its diversity its restaurants were particularly worth exploring but we did not have the time for that. What was memorable was to explore the city on foot, again walking those intriguing Portuguese pavements in the sub-tropical heat, and being revived by the São Paulo coffee vendors. The vendors were a São Paulo institution. From their sidewalk cart they served up, in tiny metal cups, *cafezinho*, a small, intense, very sweet shot of coffee made in a uniquely traditional way. The ubiquity of *cafezinho* testified to it being a cultural emblem.

While I did not have the opportunity to explore the culinary diversity of the city, I did experience the *churrasco*. This is a barbecue in the Brazilian tradition that springs from the gauchos, the cowboys of the South American grasslands. Their technique of cooking and presentation and the ambiance of the setting made the meal a truly exciting incident. At the *churrascaria* we were led to an outdoor dining area with an immense barbecue pit, about fifteen feet long. A seemingly endless array of huge skewers, fashioned as swords with cuts of meat on them near the handles, were stuck into the live charcoals. The "gaucho" cooks carefully tended the swords seeing the meat was roasted to perfection. As the cuts shed fat into the hot embers small flames would erupt along the cooking pit. First, we were served vegetables, and then a cook would approach with sword in hand to slice a custom cut for each guest. There was a superfluity of different cuts from beef, pork, and lamb, obviously an invitation to learn by return visits.

The end of our South American route was Santiago, Chili. We flew there with transit stops in Monte Video, Uruguay; and Buenos Aires, Argentina. As is well known, the western side of the South American Continent is formed by the rugged Andes Mountains which at the latitude of Santiago rise to majestic peaks higher than 20,000 feet. The Comet 4 cruising altitude in the stratosphere meant these elevations did not pose challenges to us as it had done to the Argonaut propeller aircraft that proceeded us to serve that route.[25] Top-of-descent (TOD) into Los Cerrillos Airport (now closed) was, of course, west of the mountain peaks. On flying eastward our powerful Avon engines also gave us the climb power to comfortably clear these peaks. The older aircraft had to circle in a climb configuration, and on reaching sufficient altitude fly through the mountain passes.

In Santiago, we stayed at BOAC House. This was a place that had a long association with the airline and had delighted the Argonaut crews who preceded us there. It was run by a solicitous and loyal lady, who spared no effort to make our stay feel like home-away-from-home. Our arrival on the 22 November 1960 was a reopening of the route, since the Argonauts had been withdrawn earlier. This was added cause for celebration. Dinner was to be a grand affair with the captain seated at the head of the table. There was a problem though; the heater was broken and it was apparent that the mistress of the house, due to the hiatus in the crew stopovers, did not want the expense of calling a repair crew. So I took some ribbing, "Dominic aren't you an *engineer*?"

With multilingual instructions, I made my way to a basement closet that had, I deduced, an oil-fired heater. I had zero experience of this type of equipment so all my native skills were called upon. I succeeded in lighting the pilot flame but the heater would not start. I could see the flame was directed to a thermocouple that was heavily coated in soot, so I cleaned it to the bare metal and tried again. Success! I knew the flame needed adjustment to be clean burning or it would be only a matter of time until the soot built up again. But I decided that adjusting the flame would be a "bridge too far." Besides the house had reached a lovely, comfortable temperature. I was quite pleased with myself, but the only accolades I received were, "Dominic are you sure it won't blow up?"

CHAPTER TWENTY SIX

AFTERWORD

In 1962, I was enjoying the rhythm of life: flying was a satisfying occupation, Catherine had been selected to start a social welfare agency in Northern London, and we were considering putting down roots with the purchase of an apartment in London. There were long range things to be considered though, primarily what kind of career I should pursue? My age and marital status began to make this a weightier question. There were essentially two broad paths, stay with flying and make the most of my experience or begin anew with the pursuit of a university degree. Whichever path I chose had difficulties.

In aviation, the trend was toward a crew consisting of two pilots. As noted, BOAC had attempted that in 1957, when they introduced the Bristol Britannia. It failed only because the Proteus engines had a severe problem with icing of the air intakes. Beyond that, with the tremendous increase in reliability and simplified operation of the jet engine as well as advances in systems engineering, the flight engineer's workload had decreased, making it probable that next generation of aircraft would not have flight engineers. The way forward was to undertake the expense and effort to qualify as a pilot while continuing to work. Given my heritage, the university education path beckoned strongly, but was more daunting. The correspondence courses I had pursued in County Tipperary had me complete some high school studies but I did not have a certificate.

A very timely circumstance also arose, Catherine was pregnant and would welcome loving family involvement. We did not have family close by and my job required that most of my time be spent abroad. So, we decided, and plunged ahead with my plans to chase education in the more flexible American educational institutions. I submitted my letter of resignation. An exit interview followed. I naturally had some hesitations. Given that serving had elicited a strong sense of commitment, there was a nagging feeling of disloyalty.

However, in the interview the fleet manager put me at ease with his opening comment, "Dominic remember you have not burned your boats, you will be welcome back here anytime." We then had a friendly discussion of my hopes and plans. I had a question, could I book my flights to San Francisco at the hugely advantageous BOAC employee rates? They agreed this is what I should do.

In San Francisco, working at jobs I knew were temporary was interesting. But adopting the mentality of being a student again was somewhat challenging. Gone was the sense of being at the summit of something. I worked for a period in United Airlines Maintenance Base at San Francisco Airport, rebuilding jet engines. When I read of the disaster that befell United Airlines Flight 232 in July 1989, I was acutely reminded that I had earlier worked in the very shop that had overhauled that defective engine.[26] I noted BOAC discontinued flying the Comet 4 in 1965, while numerous airlines continued to operate variants of it in passenger services until 1981.

Some of my friends went to work flying those Comet 4's for Dan Air, the English charter airline that became the operator of all of the finally airworthy Comets. The technology of the Comet was incorporated into the Sud Aviation, Caravelle, that began service in 1959 and I noted it continued in commercial operation much longer than the Comets. On a visit to England, I was excited to see a Nimrod on a landing approach. This aircraft was an extensive modification, begun in 1964, of the Comet 4. The Hawker Siddeley Nimrod was designed for marine patrol and continued in service until 2011.

In my new life, I maintained interests in aviation and avidly followed the news of developments and disasters. With satisfaction, I observed that the industry I had been immersed in continued to innovate and, arguably, become the most convenient and *safest* mode of travel.

Although it belongs to another story, I should tell here of the denouncement of my pursuit of education. In June my class at the University of California, Berkeley (UCB) in 1969 had their graduation ceremony with speeches and music in the Greek Theatre, but I graduated later *in the dean's office*. With the ardent support of Catherine, since 1963 I had worked at four jobs and studied at four institutions of higher learning. In 1966 UCB accepted my collection of study units as credits toward their program in engineering. However, they added twenty units beyond the normal requirement to compensate for my lack of a high school degree. So when my class graduated in June I could not join them. Instead I planned to petition the dean to take graduate mathematics in the Summer semester.

When I arrived in the dean's office, he knew I was an Honor student and had a department invitation to apply for graduate school. So, he questioned, "why did you not graduate?" He listened to me, but I think my explanation sounded lame to him. He would be concerned that I was contributing negatively to the vital university statistic of percent of students who graduate on time. He said rather curtly, "Sit there while I check with the records office!" He disappeared, and I sat for a while, feeling apprehensive. On returning, he cheerily announced, "I have good news and bad news. You have graduated but since you are graduated it is now too late for a graduate student to apply for the math class." I was thinking among the many cheering would be my Grandfather Thomas. He, of course, was only one of the many to whom I had reasons to be grateful.

I went on to complete a Master of Engineering degree at UCB. After graduation from there I had a career in engineering and management. In retrospect, I would not change a single iota of it.

MEET THE AUTHOR

After discharge from the Irish Air Corps I continued a career in aviation by becoming a flight engineer on the first jetliners, de Havilland Comets. The work as flight crew for BOAC was challenging as the airline developed new frontiers in aviation and new routes to exotic destinations worldwide. Returning to school, I earned an MS in Engineering from University of California, Berkeley, before working in engineering and management at various Silicon Valley companies, and as adjunct faculty at Embry Riddle University. At the heart of these work and study situations was a common focus on technology and human factors

With the changing work I published articles in, among others, *Industrial Engineer, Fidelity,* and *Wild West* magazines. In 2013, I published *The Letters of Peter H. Burnett: Realism and The Roots of California*, a biographical sketch of the first elected American governor of California. For further anecdotes and pictures, see http://www.ventureintothestratosphere.com.

ACRONYMS

Acronyms and specialist words are unavoidable when talking about aviation. Some of them may need explanation.

ATC: Air Traffic Control.

AUW: All Up Weight.

BOAC: British Overseas Airways Corporation. Successor corporation to Imperial Airways, and later incorporated into BA, British Airways.

CRM: Variously stands for "cockpit resource management" and "crew resource management."

DECCA: Long range navigation equipment by British pioneering company Decca Navigator Company Ltd.

DME: Distance Measuring Equipment. Displays the slant distance from an aircraft to a transponder on the ground.

FTL: Flight Time Limitations. National regulations on the duty time of flight crew.

GPS: Global Positioning Satellite. Navigation system.

ILS: Instrument Landing System. A radio system showing when an aircraft at altitude is on the proper glide slope and track to land on a particular runway.

JPT: Jet Pipe Temperature. (Excessive jet engine exhaust temperatures could result in structural failures!).

LORAN LOng RAnge Navigation. The equipment for use with or the various systems of Long Range Navigation implemented by American Government.

MAD: Mutually Assured Destruction. The logic 0f the Cold War deterrence of nuclear attack.

NOTAMS: Notices to Airmen. A advisory issued by an aviation authority to notify pilots of changes or hazards at airports and along flight routes.

OAT Outside Air Temperature. The ambient temperature at the aircraft.

NTSB: National Transportation Safety Board. An independent United States Federal agency.

PORT: The left side of the craft when facing forward.

PPL: Private Pilot License. An initial pilot license.

RAF: Royal Air Force (British).

RPM: Revolutions Per Minute.

SOP: Standard Operating Procedure. Often supported by a check list.

STARBOARD: The right side of the craft when facing forward.

TBO: Time Between Overhaul. Used for equipment maintenance.

TOC: Top of Climb. When the aircraft reaches its initial cruising altitude.

TOD: Top Of Descent, The point at which an aircraft leaves its cruising altitude for landing.

VOR: VHF Omni Range. Navigational radio.

V1: The speed reached by an aircraft in takeoff mode after which it cannot safely stop on the runway

V2: The speed reached by an aircraft in takeoff mode after which it can takeoff even with the loss of one engine.

WAYPOINT: A two-dimensional point in space defined by radio beams, used for aircraft navigation.

ENDNOTES

1   What we called fairy forts were prehistoric dwellings. The coun-
    try people viewed them with awe and farmers customarily farmed
    around them. In pagan thought, they were associated with the spirit
    world and fairies.

2   An obvious parallel to Ernest Hemingway's 1952 novel, *The Old Man
    and the Sea* (New York: Scribner, 1952).

3   Consider, in the thirteenth century, St. Thomas Aquinas (ST I–II,
    105,1). He said that Natural Law provides for the people to select
    and depose their rulers. Democracy is associated with Greek City
    States, but in those societies, as in Rome, citizenship was restricted
    and slavery was permissible.

4   See Mt. 22:21; 1Peter 2:13,15; Rom. 13:1–2,5; and Tertullian's *Apology*.

5   The public demonstrations are chronicled by Winston Groom in *The
    Aviators: Eddie Rickenbacker, Jimmy Doolittle, Charles Lindbergh, and
    the Epic Age of Flight* (Washington, DC: National Geographic Society,
    2013).

6   Dominic Colvert, "Initiative," *An Cosantóir* Vol. 56 Number 5 (1996):
    24–25.

7   Charles A. Lindberg, *The Spirit of St. Louis*, (St Paul: Minnesota His-
    torical Society Press, 1993).

8   https://en.wikipedia.org/United_Airlines_Flight_232. Accessed
        2016/10/9.

9   See L Ron Hubbard, *Dianetics: The Modern Science of Mental Health*
        (New York: Hermitage House, 1950).

10   Charles Frankel, *The Case for Modern Man* (Boston: Beacon
        Hill,1959). Frankel obtained his Ph.D. from Columbia in 1949 and
        was a professor of philosophy there.

11   Gerry Catling, http://betteronacamel.com. Accessed 2016/9/30.

12   The aircraft, G APDB, we flew on these sectors can still be seen in its
        BOAC livery at Duxford Aviation Society, Duxford Airfield, Dux-
        ford, Cambridgeshire, England.

13   See Chapter Nine.

14   *Roman Holiday* a delightful, light-hearted, award-winning romantic
        movie released in 1953.

15   *Far Away Places* by songwriters Joan Whitney and Alex Kramer was
        sung by many popular artists, but the dreamy, haunting rendition, by
        Bing Crosby, was probably never surpassed.

16   *The Captain's Paradise* is a 1953 British comedy film. The captain is
        the owner and skipper of a ship that ferries between Gibraltar and
        Kalique. Secretly, he has a Gibraltar wife, who is domestic, and a
        Kalique wife who is exotic; part of the comic situation is the wives'
        desire to be different— the domestic to be exotic and the exotic to be
        domestic. They both leave him for other lovers.

17   More than fifty years later, when Catherine died, I found among her
        papers the highly creased and slightly yellowed Nile Hilton stationery
        with the still fresh ideas and words I had written.

18   Gerry Catling, http://betteronacamel.com. Accessed 2016/9/30.

19   *The Bridge on the River Kwai* is a 1957 British-American epic war film

directed by David Lean and starring William Holden, Jack Hawkins, and Alec Guinness. The story follows Japanese POWs forced to build a bridge and their ambivalence when they have the opportunity to destroy their work.

20   See Chapter Nine.

21   For an interesting account of the study of Aboriginal religion and land issues in the 1950s in a town about 100 mile southwest of Darwin, see W.E.H. Stanner and John Hilary Martin, *People from the Dawn: Religion, Homeland, and Privacy in Australian Aboriginal Culture* (Antioch: Solas Press, 2001).

22   There is a concept of fairness, where negotiating parties retreat behind a "veil of ignorance," obviating the inequality of the parties. But this and other theoretical concepts, like the Enlightenment's "social contract," would have been ineffective here.

23   It was interesting to also note that the interests of the aboriginals would not be met by self-serving interests of academics. For example, an objective of the Harvard-Peabody-Expedition of 1961–1963 to Papua was in studying the Dani cannibals to see what it might say of civilized people.

24   The poem was published by William Butler Yeats, Ed., *Fairy and Folk Tales of the Irish Peasantry* (New York: Dover Publications, 1991).

25   The Argonaut was a Canadian-built Douglas DC4 that was modified for Rolls Royce Merlin engines.

26   See Chapter Nine.

Morgan James
Speakers Group

Morgan James makes all of our titles available
through the Library for All Charity Organization.

www.LibraryForAll.org

Printed in the USA
CPSIA information can be obtained
at www.ICGtesting.com
JSHW022331140824
68134JS00019B/1410